FATTY LIVER DIET COOKBOOK

365 DAYS EXPRESS & HEALTHY LOW-FAT RECIPES TO IMPROVE YOUR HEALTH AND LIVE LONGER. DISCOVER THE PERSONALIZED 28-DAY MEAL PLAN TO EFFORTLESSLY REGAIN YOUR YOUTHFUL ENERGY

Dr. Lindsay Burton

Table of Content

Introduction

The liver is the body's 2nd-largest organ. It aids in the digestion of nutrients from food and beverages and the removal of toxic chemicals from the bloodstream. Hepatic steatosis is an alternative term used for fatty liver. It happens when the liver develops a clog with fat. Small fat levels are acceptable in the liver, but too much may be harmful to your health. Too much fat in the liver can lead to inflammation, damage, and scar your liver. This scarring may lead to liver failure in severe situations.

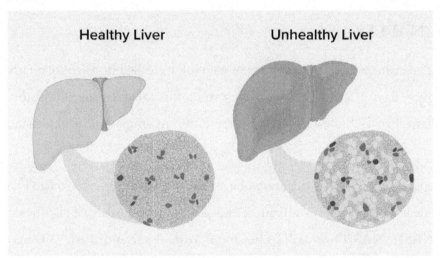

Alcoholic fatty liver disease happens when a fatty liver grows in someone who consumes a lot of alcohol (AFLD). NAFLD affects up to 25% to 30% of persons in the United States and Europe, according to a 2017 scientific review. Nonalcoholic fatty liver disease is a catch-all name for various liver diseases that afflict individuals who don't consume much alcohol. As the term indicates, NAFLD is characterized by an excess of fat deposited in liver cells.

NAFLD is becoming more frequent over the globe, particularly in Western countries. It is the most prevalent type of chronic liver disease in the United States, affecting almost one-quarter of the population. Nonalcoholic steatohepatitis (NASH) is an aggressive fatty liver disease defined by liver inflammation that may proceed to severe scarring (Cirrhosis) or liver failure in certain people with NAFLD. This harm is comparable to that induced by high alcohol consumption.

Types of Fatty Liver Disease

Fatty liver disease is divided into two types: nonalcoholic and alcoholic. Although it is unusual, fatty liver may develop during pregnancy.

Nonalcoholic fatty liver disease (NAFLD)

When fat builds up in the liver of individuals who don't consume a lot of alcohol, it's called nonalcoholic fatty liver disease (NAFLD). You may be diagnosed with NAFLD if you have extra fat in your liver and no history of severe alcohol use. The disease is referred to as basic NAFLD if there is no inflammation or associated consequences.

NAFLD involves nonalcoholic steatohepatitis (NASH). It occurs when excess fat in the liver is related to inflammation. If you have extra fat in your liver, your liver is inflamed, and you have no history of significant alcohol use, your doctor may diagnosis NASH. NASH may lead to hepatic fibrosis if left untreated. This may lead to Cirrhosis and liver failure in extreme situations.

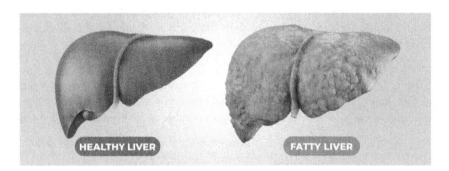

NAFLD stands for nonalcoholic fatty liver disease, which refers to a group of disorders caused by an accumulation of fat in the liver. It is more common in overweight or obese persons. Early-stage NAFLD is typically harmless, but if it progresses, it may cause severe liver damage, including Cirrhosis. High amounts of fat in the liver are linked to a higher risk of significant health issues, including diabetes, high blood pressure, and renal disease.

NAFLD raises your chances of getting cardiac issues if you already have diabetes. It is feasible to prevent NAFLD from worsening and lower the amount of fat in your liver if it is discovered and treated early on.

NAFLD progresses via four phases.

Most individuals will only ever develop the first stage, which they will normally be unaware of. If not recognized and controlled, it may worsen and lead to liver damage in a small percentage of patients.

The following are the phases of NAFLD:

1. simple fatty liver (steatosis) – a relatively innocuous accumulation of fat in the liver cells that can only be detected when tests are conducted for another cause.

2. Nonalcoholic steatohepatitis (NASH) — is a more severe variant of NAFLD in which the liver is inflamed.

3. Fibrosis - scar tissue forms around the liver and adjacent blood vessels because of continuous inflammation, but the liver continues to function properly.

4. cirrhosis – the most advanced stage, which develops after years of inflammation and causes the liver to shrink, scar, and lump; this damage is irreversible and may lead to liver failure (where your liver stops working properly) as well as liver cancer

Fibrosis and Cirrhosis may take years to develop. To keep the illness from worsening, it's critical to adopt lifestyle modifications.

Am I at risk of nonalcoholic fatty liver disease (NAFLD)?

*   have type 2 diabetes
*   have a condition that affects how your body uses insulin
*   are insulin resistance
*   have an underactive thyroid
*   have high blood pressure
*   have high cholesterol
*   have metabolic syndrome (a combination of diabetes, high blood pressure, and obesity

Symptoms of nonalcoholic fatty liver disease (NAFLD)

In the early stages of NAFLD, there are generally no symptoms. Unless it's discovered via testing for another reason, you're unlikely to realize you have it. NASH or fibrosis (more advanced stages of NAFLD) patients may have the following symptoms:

*   a dull or unbearable ache in the upper right of the belly (over the lower right side of the ribcage)
*   excessive exhaustion
*   unexplained weight loss
*   weakness

If you develop Cirrhosis (the most advanced stage), you may have more severe symptoms such as jaundice (yellowing of the skin and whites of the eyes), itching skin, and swelling in your legs, ankles, feet, or stomach (edema).

How is a nonalcoholic fatty liver disease (NAFLD) diagnosed?

After a blood test called a liver function test yields an abnormal result and other liver disorders, such as hepatitis, are ruled out, NAFLD is often diagnosed. However, blood testing may not always detect NAFLD.

An ultrasound examination of your belly may also reveal the issue. Sound waves are utilized to generate a picture of the interior of your body in this sort of scan.

If you've been diagnosed with NAFLD, you may need further testing to establish which stage you're in. This might include a particular blood test or a different sort of ultrasound exam (Fibro scan).

A biopsy, in which a tiny sample of liver tissue is obtained with a needle and analyzed in a laboratory, may be required in certain cases.

An ultrasound examination of the liver should be done every three years for children and young adults at risk of NAFLD (those with type 2 diabetes or metabolic syndrome).

A CT scan or an MRI scan are two more tests you could get.

Treatment for nonalcoholic fatty liver disease (NAFLD)

Most individuals with NAFLD will not develop significant complications, but if you've been diagnosed, it's a good idea to take action to prevent it from worsening. There is no treatment for NAFLD, although adopting healthy lifestyle choices may assist. Treatment for related disorders (high blood pressure, diabetes, and cholesterol) or consequences may also be indicated. You may be encouraged to see your doctor frequently to monitor your liver function and search for any symptoms of new disorders.

Medicines

There is presently no drug that can cure NAFLD. However, a variety of medications may help manage the symptoms of the disease. Your doctor may, for example, prescribe medication to manage high blood pressure, high cholesterol, type 2 diabetes, and obesity.

Transplantation of the liver

If you develop severe Cirrhosis and your liver stops functioning correctly, you may need to be placed on a liver transplant waiting list. Alternatively, a transplant utilizing a portion of the liver from a living donor may be viable. Because the liver can regenerate, both the transplanted piece and the remaining portion of the donor's liver may recover to their original size.

Things you can do if you have nonalcoholic fatty liver disease (NAFLD)

The most effective strategy to manage NAFLD is to adopt a healthy lifestyle.

For example, it can help you:

- lose weight – aim for a BMI of 18.5 to 24.9 (use the BMI calculator to calculate your BMI); losing more than 10% of your weight can help remove fat from the liver and improve NASH if you have it; eating smaller portions of food can also help
- drink water instead of sweet drinks
- Exercise consistently – aim for at least 150 minutes of moderate-intensity activity each week, such as walking or cycling; any exercise, regardless of weight loss, will help improve NAFLD.
- Quit smoking – if you smoke, quitting can help lower your risk of heart attacks and strokes.

Although alcohol does not cause NAFLD, it may exacerbate it. As a result, it is suggested to reduce or eliminate alcohol use.

Alcoholic Fatty Liver Disease (AFLD)

The liver is harmed by excessive alcohol use. The first stage of alcohol-related liver disease is an alcoholic fatty liver disease (AFLD). The disease is classified as simple alcoholic fatty liver if there is no inflammation or other problems.

A form of AFLD is alcoholic steatohepatitis (ASH). It occurs when excess fat in the liver is combined with inflammation, known as alcoholic hepatitis. If you have extra fat in your liver, your liver is inflamed, or you consume a lot of alcohol, your doctor may diagnose ASH.

ASH may lead to hepatic fibrosis if it isn't managed appropriately. Cirrhosis (severe scarring of the liver) may result in liver failure. The buildup of fat in the liver because of extensive drinking is known as alcoholic fatty liver. (One drink per day for women & up to two drinks per day for males is considered moderate drinking.) This kind of liver disease affects around 5% of adults in the United States.

Symptoms of alcohol-related liver disease (ARLD)

ARLD normally does not manifest itself until the liver has been extensively damaged. When this occurs, you may have the following symptoms:

- nausea
- weight loss
- lack of appetite
- jaundice (yellowing of the eyes and skin)
- swelling in the ankles and abdomen
- disorientation or sleepiness
- vomiting blood or passing blood in your stools

As a result, ARLD is commonly discovered during testing for other diseases or at an advanced stage of liver damage. Whether you consume too much alcohol regularly, notify your doctor so they can assess if your liver is affected.

Alcohol and the Liver

The liver is the most complicated organ in the body, apart from the brain. Its duties include:

- removing toxins from the blood.
- Assisting in food digestion.
- Managing blood sugar and cholesterol levels and
- assisting in the fight against infection and illness.

The liver is very robust & capable of self-regeneration. Some liver cells die every time your liver filters alcohol. The liver can regenerate new cells, but long-term alcohol abuse (drinking too much) may impair its capacity. Your liver might be permanently damaged because of this. In the United Kingdom, ARLD is frequent. Because of rising levels of alcohol abuse over the previous several decades, the number of persons with the illness has risen.

Stages of ARLD

ARLD is divided into three phases. However, there is sometimes overlap between them. These steps are described in detail below.

Fatty liver disease caused by alcoholism

Even if it's just for a few days, drinking a lot of alcohol may cause fat to build up in the liver. This is the initial stage of ARLD, known as alcoholic fatty liver disease. Fatty liver disease has few symptoms, yet it's a crucial indicator if you're consuming too much alcohol. Fatty liver disease may be cured. If you don't drink for two weeks, your liver should be back to normal.

Hepatitis caused by alcoholism

Severe alcoholic hepatitis, on the other hand, is a life-threatening condition. Many individuals in the UK die from the illness each year, and other people are only diagnosed with liver damage until their condition has progressed.

Cirrhosis

Cirrhosis is another stage of ARLD in which the liver is severely scarred. A person with Cirrhosis caused by alcohol which does not quit drinking has a less than 50% probability of surviving for another 5 years.

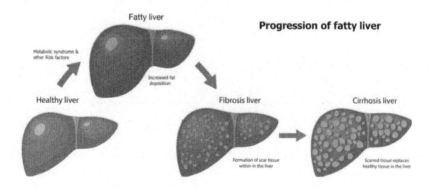

How is the alcoholic liver disease diagnosed?

Your healthcare practitioner will perform a full health history and physical examination.

- Blood tests are some of the other tests performed to identify alcohol-induced liver damage. Included are liver function tests, which determine if the liver is functioning properly.

- A biopsy of the liver. Small tissue samples are removed from the liver using a needle or during surgery. The liver illness is determined by examining these samples under a microscope.

- Ultrasound. This exam creates an image of the organs using high-frequency sound waves.

- A CT scan This imaging exam produces pictures (commonly referred to as slices) of the body using X-rays and a computer. A CT scan provides comprehensive pictures of the bones, muscles, fat, or organs in anybody section. CT scans provide more information than standard X-rays.

- MRI. MRI creates comprehensive images of inside body structures using a magnetic field, radiofrequency pulses, and a computer. Dye is sometimes injected into a vein to create photographs of bodily components. The dye aids in visualizing the liver and other abdominal organs (belly).

Treating alcohol-related liver disease (ARLD)

There is no medical therapy for ARLD currently. The most important therapy is to quit drinking for the rest of your life. This lowers the risk of future liver damage and offers your liver the greatest chance of recovery.

Stopping drinking might be tough for someone who is addicted to alcohol. However, local alcohol support agencies may be able to aid with information and medical treatment.

You will be eligible for a liver transplant if you have acquired cirrhosis issues despite quitting drinking. All liver transplant facilities ask patients to abstain from drinking alcohol for the duration of their treatment and the rest of their lives.

Complications

ARLD-related death rates have grown dramatically in recent decades. Along with smoking and high blood pressure, alcohol usage is now one of the leading causes of mortality in the United Kingdom. Internal (variceal) bleeding, toxins buildup in the brain (encephalopathy), and fluid buildup in the abdomen (ascites) with accompanying renal failure are all life-threatening consequences of ARLD.

- higher susceptibility to infection
- liver cancer
- The hepatitis C virus is found in around 30% of persons with alcoholic liver damage. Others are infected with the hepatitis B virus. Your doctor will test you for both and, if necessary, treat you.
- People who have alcoholic liver disease are more likely to get liver cancer.
- About half of the people have gallstones.
- Kidney difficulties, intestinal bleeding, fluid in the stomach, disorientation, liver cancer, and serious infections are all common symptoms of Cirrhosis.

Preventing alcohol-related liver disease (ARLD)

Stopping consuming alcohol or adhering to the suggested limits is the most effective approach to avoid ARLD:

- If you drink 14 units or more each week, spread it out across three days or more.

A unit of alcohol is about half a pint of regular beer or a pub measure of spirits (25ml). Even if you've been a heavy drinker for a long time, cutting down or quitting will have significant short- and long-term health advantages for your liver and general health.

Acute Fatty Liver of Pregnancy (AFLP)

Excess fat builds up in the liver during pregnancy, known as the acute fatty liver of pregnancy (AFLP). It's a very uncommon yet potentially fatal pregnancy condition. Although genetics might be a factor, the specific cause is uncertain.

AFLP commonly manifests itself in the third trimester of pregnancy. If left untreated, it presents major health concerns to both the mother and the baby. Your doctor will want to deliver your baby as soon as possible if your baby has AFLP. You may require follow-up care for a few days after giving birth. Within a few weeks of having delivery, your liver function should return to normal.

Foods that Cleanse the Liver

Every day, our liver works incredibly hard to shield us from the harmful effects of metabolic acid, and it is possible for our liver to get exhausted, which significantly affects our well-being.

Seven growing foods that will help you clean your liver naturally involve regular. The body transfers digestion, diet, and environmental acid through the liver to detoxify and purify the bloodstream by constantly cleansing the blood of toxins via the gastrointestinal tract, skin, and respiratory system. Yet your whole body may be thrown out of control, and your well-being is seriously impaired when your liver is overworked owing to pain or prolonged access to acid.

As the liver is also responsible for alkalizing bile development, another detox that is metabolically essential for physiological, environmental, and dietary acid break-down and removal of your lifestyle. It is necessary to alkalize the liver with an alkaline lifestyle and diet. Without a well-functioning liver, the body cannot cleanse and disinfect metabolic and dietary acid, a nutritional catastrophe receiver.

Therefore, you should start adding seven essential alkalizing foods into your diet to preserve a stable alkaline liver.

Garlic and Onion

Garlic produces a variety of sulfur-containing compounds essential for the nutrition and digestion of the body. This bulbous onion relative also includes allicin and selenium, two essential nutrients that have been shown to shield the liver from acidic damage and enable it to detoxify.

Grapefruit

Grapefruit has two effective liver cleansers, high in natural vitamin C and antioxidants. In addition, grapefruit produces compounds that balance excess acids, including garlic. This also includes a flavonoid compound named naringenin, which allows acids to bind, be absorbed in the liver, and not be retained in the fatty tissues.

Green Grasses

Green grasses are filled with chlorophyll, the fundamental molecule of green grass which buffers excess metabolic and dietary acids, including wheat and barley grass. Chlorophyll production from green grasses also helps detoxify small intestines and the liver and maintain the body alkaline.

Green Vegetables

Leafy, black, gourd, arugula, dandelion leaves, spinach, mustard greens, and chicory produce various purification compounds that neutralize heavy metals that can heavily bear on the liver. In addition, leafy greens often remove from the body pesticides and herbicides and facilitate the formation and distribution of alkaline bile cleansing.

Avocado

Rich in glutathione-producing compounds, avocados vigorously foster liver safety by the defense against and improve the healing forces against toxic acid overload. Studies have shown that consuming 1 or 2 avocados a week will heal a weakened liver for as little as 30 days. Therefore, Dr. Robert O. Young tells the doctor to consume an avocado daily.

Walnuts

Walnuts, which include high l-arginine, amino acid, glutathione, and omega-3 fatty acids, also lead to the liver's detoxification from disease-induced ammonia. In addition, walnuts often absorb oxygen, and extracts from their hulls are also used in liver purification formulae.

Turmeric

Turmeric, one of the most effective foods for healthy liver maintenance, has proven that it effectively defends the liver from oxidative damage and regenerates weakened liver cells. Turmeric also stimulates natural bile development, decreases engorged hepatic ducts, and increases the overall function of the gallbladder, another organ that purifies the blood.

Detoxing Your Body

Detoxification is the cleaning of unidentified body contaminants (toxins) and also the exclusion of body intoxicants (opioids, drugs, alcohol) until participation in something like a SUD (substance use disorders) or recovery program from addiction. They aren't the exact thing.

Uniform Alcoholism & intoxication Care Act (1971) suggested that it was better for those with an AUD (alcohol use disorders) to undergo medication instead of prosecution; detoxification became standard procedure for people with AUD (alcohol use disorder). They might "lead regular lives as community citizens" in that manner.

What Does Detox Do?

For detox work, you should avoid using harmful substance that triggers your health issues, including lead-containing materials, fatty foods, or addictive things like alcohol or narcotics. Then the liver, digestive system, kidneys, lungs, and skin of your body remove the residual contaminants, returning the body to its pre-toxin condition. The body typically needs time if it's healthy.

Some individuals claim that you will speed up the Process with an extreme diet, vigorously eliminating the toxins: supplements (natural), juicing foods, or proprietary tonics for best digestion.

Detox Full Body

In the familiar context, a cleanse or complete body detox is a way to purge the body's "toxins" (chemicals, impurities, and pollutants) to stay healthy to live happy and longer.

If you're healthy, drinking healthy fluids, sufficient water, and eating good food, then this detox type is what your body is prepared to do without any support. It's a diet. You involve vegetables and Juicing fruits, taking away toxic things (coffee, sugar, tobacco, alcohol), and exercise.

If you eat vegetables and fruits instead of refined grains, beef, sugar, and wheat, you'll lose weight, get more stamina, and feel better, so you don't have to drink those juices. You should enjoy vegetables and fruit. Good for you is the food fiber. It is needless to juice food or purchases pricey fluids containing dietary supplements.

Detoxing Misconceptions

Detox is a standard step in a balanced body and does not need attention. You will get fewer chemicals in your system once you avoid eating them, although there is no proof that diet programs quick up the method. If you have lesser toxins in the body, you will accumulate lesser toxins. Few popular misconceptions regarding detoxifying involve:

Using detox techniques would not accelerate the removal of contaminants from the system. All the so-called contaminants are not named, and there is no proof of any contaminants exiting the body sooner due to detox.

Detox regimes do not help you shed weight. Yeah, once you avoid consuming sugars, fried products, and carbs, you will likely lose fat; however, you are losing food, not pollutants. When you take diuretics and laxatives, you can lose weight in the near term, but you often run to the toilet. In addition, you may end up becoming dehydrated dangerously.

Activated charcoal would not flush out liquor. It is utilized for purifying or aeration in manufacturing operations. Some also reported this to clarify and avoid or ease cramps or even excessive drinking. Worse still, one contaminant that charcoal cannot flush off is liquor. It may inhibit the ingestion of many other compounds, but it may be the nutrients you require.

7-Day Detox Plan to Clear Your Body

Day 1-2

You should make vegetarian foods available on days 1 and 2. The vegetable can either be fresh or frozen. Either of the two does not matter. Drinking squeezed lemon juice is highly recommended if you follow the first simple practice.

Other advisable things to do, include:

· Make use of foodstuffs grown or raised without synthetic fertilizers, such as cold-pressed extra virgin olive oil.

It can be flavored with the addition of healthy aromatic vegetable substances like spices.

· Drink tea all day especially minted tea. It will help to increase bile secretion and encourage bile flow, which helps to speed and ease digestion

· Take in well-filtered water of about 6 to 11 glassfuls.

· Top this up with smoothies and diluted juices. The sugar strength, if present, must be meager.

· Have mixed nuts, vegetables, and fruits for noshes or snacks.

· You should exercise for about an hour or half an hour. It could be jogging, a long walk, bicycling, jumping, etc.

· Make yourself address and detox your mental self customary. Take some deep breaths and some minutes of meditation twice a day.

· Having steam room therapy will have beneficial effects on your cardiovascular system. It would help if you considered this as an option.

· Get some rest. This should relax your body and refresh your entire body system.

Day 3

You should eliminate any form of meat on Day 3. Do away also with rice, beans, and any non-vegetal edibles. You should take vegetables and fruits even in a more significant amount. The vegetables should be healthily prepared, and the fruits must be well washed.

You can equally introduce some practices of Days 1 and 2, such as:

- Healthy aromatic vegetable substances like spices and seasonings as well
- Herbal supplements intake (optional)
- Carry out an abstemious exercise of your body
- Drink well-filtered water, diluted juice, and even smoothies
- Get some rest and try to meditate
- Take in minted tea

Additionally, massage therapy is recommended on Day 3. It manipulates the body and relaxes the entire system.

Day 4

At this point, you should disassociate yourself from any solid food. Hydrate your body by drinking lots of water, diluted juices, and even smoothies. On Day 4, you must be attentive to your body for any changes. You should also consider:

- Plenty of intake of herbal teas
- Rest enough, and relax your bones. Do not exercise, and if at all you feel it is necessary to exercise, you are to avoid heavy workouts
- A quick nap and meditate for like 15 – 20 minutes
- Like in the second point of this list, avoid hard work. If you must do anything, it should be very minimal or take the least possible action.
- Take in lots of fluids to help hydrate and regulate your body system.

- Bowel Cleansing Regimen (Optional)
- On this day of reduced or no food intake, you should take Bentonite Clay of about 500 – 1000 mg.
- For bowel elimination, you should drink 300 mL of Magnesium Citrate in the morning.

Day 5

(This practice will be the same as on Day 3) This day is when you reintroduce fruits, vegetables, and other vegetal foods. Take them in any quantity that suits you. You can have them frozen, dried, or fresh. Be sure to prepare them healthily to support the body tissues. You do not require any unique or new activity on this day. All you need now is to reinvent the operations on Days 1 to 3.

You can also include energy work sessions to help relax and balance your body.

Days 6- 7

(Similar to Days 1 and 2) You can also collect mushrooms, legumes, beans, and other healthy grains. Continue with the intake of vegetarian foods.

The below-mentioned activities are also recommended, just as for day 1:

- Use virgin olive oil
- Healthy aromatic vegetable substances like spices and healthy seasonings
- Perform light exercises
- Drink well-filtered water, mixed juice, and even smoothies healthily made
- Take mixed nuts, vegetables, and fruits for noshes or snacks
- Have steam room therapy for the benefit of your cardiovascular system
- Journaling or medication
- Have mixed nuts, vegetables, and fruits for noshes or snacks

BREAKFAST RECIPES

1. Kamut Porridge

Preparation Time: 5 minutes
Cooking Time: 10 minutes
Ingredients:
- ½ cup Kamut
- ¼ teaspoon salt
- 2 tablespoons agave syrup
- ½ tablespoon coconut oil
- 2 cups walnut milk, homemade

Directions:
1. Plug in a high-speed food processor or blender, add Kamut in its jar, and then pulse until cracked.
2. Take a medium saucepan, add Kamut in it along with salt, pour in the milk and then stir until combined.
3. Place the pan over high heat, bring the mixture to boil, then switch heat to medium-low level and simmer for 5 to 10 minutes until thickened to the desired level.
4. Then remove the pan from heat, stir agave syrup and oil into the porridge and then distribute evenly between two bowls.
5. Garnish the porridge with diet approved fruits and then serve.

Nutrition: 183 Calories; 2 g Fats; 10 g Protein; 30 g Carbohydrates; 4 g Fiber;

2. Zucchini Pancakes

Preparation Time: 10 minutes
Cooking Time: 8 minutes

Servings: 2
Ingredients:
- 1 cup spelt flour
- ½ cup grated zucchini
- ¼ cup chopped walnuts
- 1 cup walnut milk, homemade
- Extra:
- 1 tablespoon date
- 1 tablespoon grapeseed oil

Directions:
1. Take a medium bowl, place flour in it, add date, and then stir until mixed.
2. Add mashed burro banana and milk in it, whisk until smooth batter comes together, and then fold in nuts and zucchini until just mixed.
3. Take a large skillet pan, place it over medium-high heat, add oil and when hot, pour the batter in it in portion and then shape each portion into a pancake.
4. Cook each pancake for 3 to 4 minutes per side and then serve.

Nutrition: 130 Calories; 4 g Fats; 3 g Protein; 21 g Carbohydrates; 3 g Fiber;

3. Spelt Pancakes

Preparation Time: 10 minutes
Cooking Time: 6 minutes
Ingredients:
- ½ cup spelt flour
- 1/4 cup mashed burro banana
- ¼ cup and 2 tablespoons walnut milk, homemade
- ½ teaspoon date
- 1 ½ teaspoons key lime juice
- Extra:
- 1 tablespoon grapeseed oil
- 1 ½ teaspoon walnut butter, homemade

Directions:
1. Take a medium bowl, pour in milk, stir in lime juice, let it rest for 5 minutes and then whisk in butter and mashed burro banana until combined.
2. Take a separate medium bowl, place flour in it, stir in
3. and then whisk in milk mixture until smooth.
4. Take a large skillet pan, place it over medium-high heat, add oil, and when hot, ladle the batter in it in four portions, shape each portion into a pancake and then cook for 2 to 3 minutes per side until golden brown and cooked.

Nutrition: 103.4 Calories; 1.6 g Fats; 7 g Protein; 23.1 g

Carbohydrates; 3.5 g Fiber;

4. Burro banana Nut Muffin

Preparation Time: 10 minute
Cooking Time: 20 minutes
Ingredients:
- 1 burro banana, peeled, mashed
- ¾ cup spelt flour
- ½ burro banana, peeled, cut into chunks
- 6 tablespoons date
- 6 tablespoons walnut milk, homemade
- Extra:
- ¼ teaspoon of sea salt
- ½ tablespoon key lime juice
- 2 tablespoons grapeseed oil
- ¼ cup chopped walnuts

Directions:
1. Switch on the oven, then set it to 400 degrees F and let it preheat.
2. Meanwhile, take a medium bowl, place all the dry Ingredients: in it and then stir until mixed.
3. Then a separate bowl, place the mashed burro banana in it, add all the wet Ingredients:, whisk until combined, and then whisk in flour mixture until smooth.
4. Fold in nuts and burro banana pieces and then spoon the mixture evenly into four muffin cups.
5. Bake the muffins for 15 to 20 minutes until firm and cooked and then serve.

Nutrition: 204.1 Calories; 8.5 g Fats; 3.3 g Protein; 30 g Carbohydrates; 1.4 g Fiber;

5. Crunchy Alkaline Breakfast Bars

Preparation Time: 10 minute
Cooking Time: 10 minutes
Ingredients:
- ½ cup spelt flour
- 2 baby burro bananas
- 1 cup quinoa flakes
- 1/16 teaspoon sea salt
- 1 tablespoon agave nectar
- Extra:
- ¼ cup grapeseed oil
- ½ cup alkaline blackberry jam

Directions:
1. Switch on the oven, then set it to 350 degrees F and let it preheat.

2. Meanwhile, place peeled burro bananas in a medium bowl and then mash by using a fork.
3. Add agave nectar and oil, stir until well combined, and then stir in salt, flour, and quinoa flakes until a sticky dough comes together.
4. Take a square dish, line it with parchment sheet, spread two-third of the prepared dough in its bottom, layer with blackberry jam, and then top with remaining dough.
5. Bake for 10 minutes and then let the dough cool for 15 minutes.
6. Cut the dough into four bars and then serve.

Nutrition: 108.6 Calories; 3 g Fats; 1.6 g Protein; 19.4 g Carbohydrates; 1.6 g Fiber;

6. Breakfast Herbal Smoothie

Preparation Time: 5 minutes
Cooking Time: 0 minutes
Ingredients:
- 2 cups Herbal Tea
- 1 burro banana, peeled
- 1 tablespoon walnut
- 1 tablespoon agave syrup

Directions:
1. Plug in a high-speed food processor or blender and add all the Ingredients: in its jar.
2. Cover the blender jar with its lid and then pulse for 40 to 60 seconds until smooth.
3. Divide the drink between two glasses and then serve.

Nutrition: 75.5 Calories; 2.1 g Fats; 0.9 g Protein; 13.2 g Carbohydrates; 1.8 g Fiber;

7. Quinoa Porridge with Amaranth

Preparation Time: 5 minutes
Cooking Time: 15 minutes
Serve: 2
Ingredients:
- ½ cup amaranth, cooked
- 2 tablespoons agave syrup
- ½ cup black quinoa, cooked
- ½ cup soft-jelly coconut milk
- 2 cups spring water

Directions:
1. Take a medium saucepan, place it over medium heat, add cooked quinoa and amaranth, pour in the water, stir until mixed, and then bring it a boil.

2. Switch heat to the low level and then simmer for 10 to 25 minutes until grains have absorbed all the liquid.
3. Pour in the milk, add agave syrup, stir until mixed, and then simmer for another 5 minutes until thoroughly cooked and slightly thickened.

Nutrition: 204 Calories; 4 g Fats; 8 g Protein; 33 g Carbohydrates; 3 g Fiber;

8. Zucchini Bread Pancakes

Preparation Time: 10 minutes
Cooking Time: 8 minutes
Ingredients
- 1 cup spelt flour
- ½ cup grated zucchini
- ¼ cup chopped walnuts
- 1 cup walnut milk, homemade
- Extra:
- 1 tablespoon date sugar
- 1 tablespoon grapeseed oil

Directions
1. Take a medium bowl, place flour in it, add date sugar, and then stir until mixed.
2. Add mashed banana and milk in it, whisk until smooth batter comes together, and then fold in nuts and zucchini until just mixed.
3. Take a large skillet, place over medium-high heat, add oil and when hot, pour the batter in it in portion and then shape each portion into a pancake.
4. Cook each pancake for 3 to 4 minutes per side and then serve.
5. Storage instructions:
6. Cool the pancakes, divide evenly between two meal prep containers, cover with a lid, and then store the containers in the refrigerator for up to 7 days.
7. Storage instructions:
8. When ready to eat, reheat in the oven for 1 to 2 minutes until hot and then serve.

Nutrition: 130 Calories; 4 g Fats; 3 g Protein; 21 g Carbohydrates; 3 g Fiber;

9. Blueberry Spelt Pancakes

Preparation Time: 10 minutes
Cooking Time: 8 minutes
Ingredients:
- 1 cup spelt flour
- ¼ cup blueberries

- ¼ cup agave syrup
- 1/8 teaspoon sea moss
- ½ cup soft-jelly coconut milk
- Extra:
- ¼ cup spring water
- 2 tablespoons grapeseed oil

Directions:
1. Take a large bowl, place flour in it, add agave syrup, 1 tablespoon oil and sea moss, and then stir until mixed.
2. Whisk in milk and water until smooth batter comes together and then fold in berries.
3. Take a large skillet pan, place it over medium heat, add remaining oil and when hot, ladle batter in it, shape into a pancake and then cook for 2 to 3 minutes per side until golden brown and cooked.

Nutrition: 156 Calories; 3.6 g Fats; 8.4 g Protein; 22.8 g Carbohydrates; 3.3 g Fiber;

10. Cardamom and Apple Quinoa Porridge

Preparation Time: 10 minutes
Cooking Time: 20 minutes
Servings: 2
Ingredients:
- 1 cup quinoa
- 4 cardamom pods
- 2 apples, cut into slices
- 1 teaspoon agave syrup
- 8 1/2 oz. almond milk

Directions:
1. Add cardamom and quinoa to a pan with 9 oz. water and 3 1/2 oz. milk. Bring to a boil and cook for 15 minutes.
2. Add the remaining milk and cook for 5 minutes. Remove the cardamom pods, divide the mixture among bowls and add peaches and agave syrup. Serve and

Nutrition: Calories 501 Fat 10g, Fiber 2g, Carbohydrates 18g, Protein 17

11. Arugula and Avocado Breakfast Sandwich

Preparation Time: 10 minutes
Cooking Time: 20 minutes
Servings: 2
Ingredients:

- ¼ cup almond yogurt
- 4 slices spelt flour bread, toasted
- 1 cup arugula
- 1 avocado, peeled, pitted and sliced
- 1 tablespoon pepitas
- salt and pepper

Directions:
1. Season yogurt with salt and pepper.
2. Place 2 bread slices on 2 plates. Add an even layer of yogurt sauce on the toast.
3. Add a portion of arugula and avocado on top, along with pepitas. Top with another bread slice. Slice sandwich.
4. Once done, serve.

Nutrition: Calories 132 Fat 8g, Fiber 2g, Carbohydrates 8g, Protein 8g

12.Cinnamon and Almond Porridge

Preparation Time: 10 minutes
Cooking Time: 30 minutes
Servings: 4
Ingredients:
- 2 cups almond milk
- 2 cups water
- 2 teaspoons agave syrup
- 2 cups amaranth
- ¼ teaspoon vanilla extract
- ½ cup almonds
- ½ teaspoon ground cinnamon
- ¼ teaspoon salt

Directions:
1. Add all Ingredients: except almonds and cinnamon to a pan and heat over medium heat, and stir well. Bring the mixture to a simmer. Cook for 5 minutes, stirring often.
2. Add almonds and cinnamon on top.
3. Once done, serve.

Nutrition: Calories 108, Fat 8g, Fiber 2g, Carbohydrates 8g, Protein 7g

13.Green Almond Smoothie

Preparation Time: 5 minutes
Cooking Time: 0 minutes
Servings: 1
Ingredients:
- 1 banana, frozen
- 1 cup coconut milk, unsweetened

- ¼ cup or 1 scoop Protein powder
- 2 tablespoons almond butter
- 2 cups kale
- 1 cup ice

Directions:
1. Add all the Ingredients: for the smoothie to a blender and blend until smooth.
2. Pour into chilled glasses and serve immediately.

Nutrition: Calories 340, Fat 8g, Fiber 2g, Carbohydrates 8g, Protein 6g

14.Almond Flour Muffins

Preparation Time: 10 minutes
Cooking Time: 30 minutes
Servings: 12
Ingredients:
- 1 cup blanched almond flour
- 2 flax eggs
- 1 tablespoon agave nectar
- ¼ teaspoon baking soda
- ½ teaspoon apple cider vinegar

Directions:
1. Mix soda and flour in a bowl. Mix flax eggs, nectar, and vinegar in a separate bowl.
2. Combine both mixtures and stir well.
3. Preheat the oven to 350 F, pour the mixture into muffin tins. Bake for 15 minutes.

Nutrition: Calories 108, Fat 50g, Fiber 2g, Carbohydrates 8g, Protein 48g

15.Roasted Red Rose Potatoes and Kale Breakfast Hash

Preparation Time: 10 minutes
Cooking Time: 45 minutes
Servings: 2
Ingredients:
- 2 tablespoons coconut oil, melted
- 2 red rose potatoes
- 1 teaspoon coconut
- 1 red onion, skin and tops removed and sliced into wedges lengthwise
- 1/8 teaspoon ground turmeric
- 1 bundle kale, chopped and large stems removed
- ½ teaspoon each salt and pepper
- 2 tablespoons fresh parsley

Directions:

1. Season red rose potatoes with ½ tablespoon oil, coconut
2. , and pinch salt and pepper. Toss to coat. Bake onions and potatoes for 35 minutes, flipping halfway. Remove from oven and set aside.
3. Add pressed tofu in a bowl and crumble into small pieces. Season with turmeric, parsley, a pinch of salt and pepper. Set aside.
4. Heat a skillet over medium-high heat. Add tofu, ½ tablespoon oil, and 1 teaspoon tandoori masala spice. Cook for 5 minutes, stirring occasionally. Remove from skillet and set aside.
5. Add remaining ½ tablespoon oil to the skillet and add kale in it. Season with 1 teaspoon tandoori masala spice, salt, and pepper. Cook for 4 minutes, stirring frequently.
6. Push kale to one side of the pan and add tofu to warm. Turn heat off but keep over the burner.
7. Divide kale between 2 plates and top with onion, roasted red rose potatoes. Add remaining parsley on top. Serve.

Nutrition: Calories 200, Fat 8g, Fiber 2g, Carbohydrates 8g, Protein 6g

16. Date and Almond Porridge

Preparation Time: 10 minutes
Cooking Time: 10 minutes
Servings: 1
Ingredients:
- 1 Medjool date, chopped
- 6 ¾ oz. almond milk
- 1 teaspoon almond butter
- ½ cup buckwheat flakes
- ¼ cup strawberries, hulled

Directions:
1. Add the date and milk to a pan. Heat gently and add the buckwheat flakes and cook for a few minutes.
2. Add in butter and top with strawberries. Serve.

Nutrition: Calories 200, Fat 8g, Fiber 2g, Carbohydrates 8g, Protein 6g

17. Red Rose Potato Toasts

Preparation Time: 10 minutes
Cooking Time: 15 minutes
Servings: 7
Ingredients:
- 1 tablespoon avocado oil
- 2 red rose potatoes, sliced

- 1 teaspoon salt

Directions:
1. Preheat the oven to 425 F and line a baking sheet with parchment paper.
2. Place potato slices on the parchment paper with spaces in between and grease with avocado oil on both sides.
3. Add salt on top. Bake for 5 minutes, flip and bake for 5 more minutes.

Nutrition: Calories 104, Fat 8g, Fiber 2g, Carbohydrates 8g, Protein 2.5g

18. Raspberry Smoothie Bowl

Preparation Time: 10 minutes
Cooking Time: 10 minutes
Servings: 2
Ingredients:
- 3 cups fresh raspberries, divided
- 2 frozen burro bananas, peeled
- ½ cup homemade walnut milk
- 1 tablespoon hemp seeds

Directions:
1. In a blender, add the raspberries, bananas, and walnut milk and pulse until smooth.
2. Transfer the smoothie into two serving bowls evenly.
3. Top each bowl with berries and serve immediately.

Nutrition: Calories 232 Fats 0.4 g Cholesterol 0 mg Carbohydrates 49.7 g Fiber 15.4 g Protein 5 g

19. Apple Porridge

Preparation Time: 10 minutes
Cooking Time: 5 minutes
Servings: 4
Ingredients:
- 2 cups unsweetened hemp milk
- 3 tablespoons walnuts, chopped
- 3 tablespoons sunflower seeds
- 2 large apples; peeled, cored, and grated
- Pinch of ground cinnamon
- ½ small apple, cored and sliced

Directions:
1. In a large pan, mix together the milk, walnuts, sunflower seeds, grated apple, vanilla, and cinnamon over medium-low heat and cook for about 3–5 minutes.

2. Remove from the heat and transfer the porridge into serving bowls.
3. Top with remaining apple slices and serve.

Nutrition: Calories 147 Fats 0.6 g Cholesterol 0 mg Carbohydrates 17 g Fiber 3.3 g Protein 3.2 g

20.   Cinnamon Almond Porridge

Preparation Time: 5 Minutes

Cooking Time: 5 Minutes

Servings: 1

Ingredients:
- 1 Tablespoon butter
- 1 Tablespoon coconut flour
- 1 large egg, whisked
- 1/8 teaspoon ground cinnamon
- A pinch of salt
- ¼ cup canned coconut milk
- 1 Tablespoon almond butter

Directions:

1. Melt the butter into a small saucepan over low heat.
2. Whisk the coconut flour with sugar, egg, cinnamon, and salt.
3. Remove the coconut milk while whisking, and stir in the almond butter until smooth.
4. Simmer over low heat, always stirring until heated through.
5. Spoon, then serve in a bowl.

Nutrition:
- Calories: 470
- Fat: 42g
- Protein: 13g
- Carbohydrates: 15g
- Fiber: 8g
- Net carbohydrates: 7g

21. Creamy Chocolate Protein Smoothie

Preparation Time: 5 Minutes

Cooking Time: 0 Minutes

Servings: 1

Ingredients:
- 1 cup unsweetened almond milk
- ½ Cup full-fat yogurt, plain
- ¼ Cup chocolate egg white protein powder
- 1 Tablespoon coconut oil
- 1 Tablespoon unsweetened cocoa powder
- Liquid stevia extract, to taste

Directions:

1. In a blender, add the almond milk, yogurt, and protein powder.

2. Pulse several times on the ingredients, then add the rest and blend until smooth.

3. Pour into a big glass, and instantly enjoy it.

Nutrition:
- Calories: 345
- Fat: 22g
- Protein: 29g
- Carbohydrates: 12g
- Fiber: 3g
- Net carbs: 9g

22.   Almond Butter Muffins

Preparation Time: 10 Minutes

Cooking Time: 25 Minutes

Servings: 6

Ingredients:
- 1 cup almond flour
- 1/2 cup powdered erythritol
- 1 teaspoons baking powder
- ¼ Teaspoon salt
- ¾ Cup almond butter, warmed

- ¾ Cup unsweetened almond milk
- 2 large eggs

Directions:

1. Preheat the oven to 350°F, and line a paper liner muffin pan.
2. In a mixing bowl, whisk the almond flour and the erythritol, baking powder, and salt.
3. Whisk the almond milk, almond butter, and eggs together in a separate bowl.
4. Drop the wet ingredients into the dry until just mixed together.
5. Spoon the batter into the prepared pan and bake for 22 to 25 minutes until a knife inserted in the middle comes out clean.
6. Cook the muffins in the pan for 5 minutes. Then, switch onto a cooling rack with wire.

Nutrition:
- Calories: 135
- Fat: 11g
- Protein: 6g
- Carbohydrates: 4g
- Fiber: 2g
- Net carbs: 2g

23. Almond Butter Protein Smoothie

Preparation Time: 5 Minutes

Cooking Time: 0 Minutes

Servings: 1

Ingredients:
- 1 cup unsweetened almond milk
- ½ Cup full-fat yogurt, plain
- ¼ Cup vanilla egg white protein powder
- 1 Tablespoon almond butter
- Pinch ground cinnamon
- Liquid stevia extract, to taste

Directions:
1. In a blender, add the almond milk and yogurt.
2. Pulse several times over the ingredients.
3. Stir in the remaining ingredients and blend until smooth.
4. Pour into a big glass, and instantly enjoy it.

Nutrition:
- Calories: 315
- Fat: 16,5g
- Protein: 31,5g
- Carbohydrates: 12g
- Sugar: 2,5g
- Net carb: 9,5g

24. Kale Avocado Smoothie

Preparation Time: 5 Minutes

Cooking Time: 0 Minutes

Servings: 1

Ingredients:
- 1 cup fresh chopped kale
- ½ cup chopped avocado
- ¾ Cup unsweetened almond milk
- ¼ Cup full-fat yogurt, plain
- 3 to 4 Ice cubes
- 1 Tablespoon fresh lemon juice
- Liquid stevia extract, to taste

Directions:

1. Combine the kale, avocado, and almond milk in a blender.
2. Pulse the ingredients several times.
3. Add the remaining ingredients and blend them until smooth.
4. Pour into a large glass and enjoy immediately.

Nutrition:
- Calories: 250
- Fat: 19g
- Protein: 6g
- Carbs: 17.5g
- Fiber: 6.5g
- Net carbs: 11g

25. Beets and Blueberry Smoothie

Preparation Time: 5 Minutes

Cooking Time: 0 Minutes

Servings: 1

Ingredients:

- 1 cup unsweetened coconut milk
- ¼ Cup heavy cream
- ¼ Cup frozen blueberries
- 1 small beet, peeled and chopped
- 1 Teaspoon chia seeds
- Liquid stevia extract, to taste

Directions:

1. In a blender, add the blueberries, beets, and coconut milk.
2. Pulse several times over the ingredients.
3. Stir in the remaining ingredients and blend until smooth.
4. Pour into a big glass, and instantly enjoy it.

Nutrition:

- Calories: 215
- Fat: 17g
- Protein: 2.5g
- Carbohydrates: 15g
- Fiber: 5g
- Net carbs: 10g

26. Classic Western Omelet

Preparation Time: 5 Minutes

Cooking Time: 10 Minutes

Servings: 1

Ingredients:

- 2 teaspoons coconut oil
- 3 large eggs, whisked
- 1 Tablespoon heavy cream
- Salt and pepper
- ¼ cup diced green pepper
- ¼ cup diced yellow onion
- ¼ cup diced ham

Directions:

1. In a small bowl, whisk the eggs, heavy cream, salt, and pepper.

2. Heat 1 teaspoon of coconut oil over medium heat in a small skillet.
3. Add the peppers and onions, then sauté the ham for 3 to 4 minutes.
4. Spoon the mixture in a cup, and heat the skillet with the remaining oil.
5. Pour in the whisked eggs and cook until the egg's bottom begins to set.
6. Tilt the pan and cook until almost set to spread the egg.
7. Spoon the ham and veggie mixture over half of the omelet and turn over.
8. Let the omelet cook until the eggs are set, and then serve hot.

Nutrition:

- Calories: 415
- Fat: 32,5g
- Protein: 25g
- Carbs: 6,5g
- Sugar: 1,5g
- Net carbs: 5g

27. Crispy Chai Waffles

Preparation Time: 10 Minutes

Cooking Time: 20 Minutes

Servings: 4

Ingredients:

- 4 large eggs, separated into whites and yolks
- 3 Tablespoons coconut flour
- 3 Tablespoons powdered erythritol
- 1 ¼ Teaspoon baking powder
- 1 teaspoon vanilla extract
- ½ Teaspoon ground cinnamon
- ¼ Teaspoon ground ginger
- Pinch ground cloves
- Pinch ground cardamom
- 3 Tablespoons coconut oil, melted
- 3 Tablespoons unsweetened almond milk

Directions:

1. Divide the eggs into two separate mixing bowls.
2. Whip the whites of the eggs until stiff peaks develop and then set aside.
3. Whisk the egg yolks into the other bowl with the coconut flour, erythritol, baking powder, cocoa, vanilla, cinnamon, cardamom, and cloves.
4. Pour the melted coconut oil and the almond milk into the second bowl and whisk.
5. Fold softly in the whites of the egg until you have just combined.
6. Preheat waffle iron with cooking spray and grease.
7. Spoon into the iron for about 1/2 cup of batter.
8. Cook the waffle according to directions from the maker.
9. Move the waffle to a plate and repeat with the leftover batter.

Nutrition:
- Calories: 215
- Fat: 17g
- Protein: 8g
- Carbohydrates: 8g
- Fiber: 4g
- Net carbs: 4g

28. Strawberry Rhubarb Pie Smoothie

Preparation Time: 5 Minutes

Cooking Time: 0 Minutes

Servings: 1

Ingredients:
- 1 Small stalk rhubarb, sliced
- ¼ Cup frozen sliced strawberries
- ¾ Cup unsweetened cashew milk
- ½ Cup full-fat yogurt, plain
- 1-ounce raw almonds
- ½ Teaspoon vanilla extract
- Liquid stevia extract, to taste

Directions:

1. In a blender, add the rhubarb, strawberry, and cashew milk.
2. Pulse several times over the ingredients.
3. Stir in the remaining ingredients and blend until smooth.
4. Pour into a big glass, and instantly enjoy it.

Nutrition:
- Calories: 285
- Fat: 20g
- Protein: 11g
- Carbohydrates: 17.5g
- Fiber: 5g
- Net carbs: 12. 5g

29. Bacon Mushroom and Swiss Omelet

Preparation Time: 5 Minutes

Cooking Time: 10 Minutes

Servings: 1

Ingredients:
- 3 large eggs, whisked
- 1 Tablespoon heavy cream
- Salt and pepper
- 2 slices uncooked bacon, chopped
- ¼ cup diced mushrooms
- ¼ cup shredded Swiss cheese

Directions:

- Whisk the eggs together in a small bowl with heavy cream, salt, and pepper.
- Cook the bacon over medium to high heat in a small skillet.
- Spoon it in a mug when the bacon is crisp.
- Steam the skillet over medium heat, then add the chestnuts.
- Cook the mushrooms until they smoke, then spoon the bacon into the dish.
- Heat the skillet with the remaining oil.

- Pour in the whisked eggs, and cook until the egg's bottom begins to set.
- Take a medium bowl, place the mango pieces in it, add onion, tomatoes, cucumber, and bell pepper and then drizzle with lime juice.
- Season with salt and cayenne pepper, toss until combined, and let the salad rest in the refrigerator for a minimum of 20 minutes.
- To scatter the egg, tilt the saucepan and cook until almost set.
- Spoon the mixture of bacon and mushroom over half of the omelet, then sprinkle with the cheese and fold over.
- Let the omelet cook until the eggs have been set, and serve hot.

Nutrition:
- Calories: 475
- Fat: 36g
- Protein: 34g

30. <u>Cucumber and Arugula Salad</u>

Preparation Time: 5 minutes
Cooking Time: 0 minutes
Servings: 2
Nutrition: 142 Calories; 12.5 g Fats; 1.6 g Protein; 7.8 g Carbohydrates; 1 g Fiber;
Ingredients
- ½ of cucumber, deseeded
- 4 ounces arugula
- 1/8 teaspoon salt
- 1 tablespoon key lime juice
- 1 tablespoon olive oil
- Extra:
- 1/8 teaspoon cayenne pepper

Directions
1. Cut the cucumber into slices, add to a salad bowl and then add arugula in it.
2. Mix together lime juice and oil until combined, pour over the salad, and then season with salt and cayenne pepper.
3. Toss until mixed and then serve.
4. Storage instructions:
5. Divide the salad evenly between two containers, cover with a lid, and then store the containers in the refrigerator for up to 5 days.

Nutrition: 142 Calories; 12.5 g Fats; 1.6 g Protein; 7.8 g Carbohydrates; 1 g Fiber;

SOUP, STEW, AND SAUCES

31. Zoodle Vegetable Soup

Preparation Time: 5 minutes
Cooking Time: 12 minutes
Servings: 2
Ingredients:

- ½ of onion, peeled, cubed
- ½ of green bell pepper, chopped
- ½ of zucchini, grated
- 4 ounces sliced mushrooms, chopped
- ½ cup cherry tomatoes
- Extra:
- ¼ cup basil leaves
- 1 pack of spelt noodles, cooked
- ¼ teaspoon salt
- 1/8 teaspoon cayenne pepper
- ½ of key lime, juiced
- 1 tablespoon grapeseed oil

- 2 cups spring water

Directions:

1. Take a medium saucepan, place it over medium heat, add oil and when hot, add onion and then cook for 3 minutes or more until tender.
2. Add cherry tomatoes, bell pepper, and mushrooms, stir until mixed, and then continue cooking for 3 minutes until soft.
3. Add grated zucchini, season with salt, cayenne pepper, pour in the water, and then bring the mixture to a boil.
4. Then switch heat to the low level, add cooked noodles and then simmer the soup for 5 minutes.
5. When done, ladle soup into two bowls, top with basil leaves, drizzle with lime juice and then serve.

Nutrition: 265 Calories; 2 g Fats; 4 g Protein; 57 g Carbohydrates; 13.6 g Fiber;

32. Cucumber and Basil Gazpacho

Preparation Time: 5 minutes
Cooking Time: 0 minutes
Ingredients:

- 1 avocado, peeled, pitted, cold
- 1 cucumber, deseeded, unpeeled, cold
- ½ cup basil leaves, cold
- ½ of key lime, juiced
- 2 cups spring water, chilled
- Extra:
- 1 ½ teaspoon sea salt

Directions:

1. Place all the Ingredients: into the jar of a high-speed food processor or blender and then pulse until smooth.
2. Tip the soup into a medium bowl and then chill for a minimum of 1 hour.
3. Divide the soup evenly between two bowls, top with some more basil and then serve.

Nutrition: 190 Calories; 15 g Fats; 4 g Protein; 15 g Carbohydrates; 6 g Fiber;

33. Spicy Soursop and Zucchini Soup

Preparation Time: 5 minutes
Cooking Time: 45 minutes
Servings: 2
Ingredients:

- 1 cup chopped kale
- 2 Soursop leaves, rinsed, rip in half
- ½ cup summer squash cubes
- 1 cup chayote squash cubes
- ½ cup zucchini cubes
- Extra:
- ½ cup wild rice
- ½ cup diced white onions
- 1 cup diced green bell peppers
- 2 teaspoons sea salt
- ½ tablespoon basil
- ¼ teaspoon cayenne pepper
- ½ tablespoon oregano
- 6 cups spring water

Directions:
1. Take a medium pot, place it over medium-high heat, add soursop leaves, pour in 1 ½ cup water, and then boil for 15 minutes, covering the pan with lid.
2. When done, remove eaves from the broth, switch heat to medium level, add remaining Ingredients: into the pot, stir until mixed, and then cook for 30 minutes or more until done.

Nutrition: 224 Calories; 5 g Fats; 5.8 g Protein; 38.1 g Carbohydrates; 3.4 g Fiber;

34. Delicious Chickpea & Mushroom Bowl

Preparation Time: 5 minutes
Cooking Time: 10 minutes
Servings: 2
Ingredients:
- 1 ½ cup cooked chickpeas
- 2 zucchinis, spiralized
- 4 small oyster mushrooms, destemmed, diced
- ¼ of white onion, peeled, chopped
- ¼ of red bell pepper, cored, chopped
- Extra:
- 1/3 teaspoon sea salt; 1 teaspoon dried basil
- ¼ teaspoon cayenne pepper; 1 teaspoon dried oregano
- 1 tablespoon grapeseed oil
- 2 ½ cups vegetable broth, homemade

Directions:
1. Take a medium pot, place it over medium-high heat, add oil and when hot, add red pepper, onion,

and mushrooms, season with salt and cayenne pepper, and then cook for 5 minutes until tender.
2. Switch heat to medium-low level, add remaining Ingredients: except for zucchini noodles, stir until mixed, and then simmer the soup for 15 to 20 minutes.
3. Then add zucchini noodles into the pan, stir until mixed, and then cook for 1 minute or more until thoroughly warmed.

Nutrition: 242 Calories; 9 g Fats; 10 g Protein; 34 g Carbohydrates; 9 g Fiber;

35. Zoodle Chickpea Soup

Preparation Time: 5 minutes
Cooking Time: 25 minutes
Servings: 2
Ingredients:
- ½ cup cooked, chickpeas
- ½ of a medium white onion, peeled, diced
- ½ of a large zucchini, chopped
- 1 cup kale leaves
- 1 cup squash cubes
- Extra:
- ¾ teaspoon salt
- ¾ tablespoon chopped thyme, fresh
- ¾ tablespoon tarragon, fresh
- 2 cups vegetable broth, homemade
- 1 ½ cup spring water

Directions:
1. Take a saucepan, place it over medium-high heat, pour in the ¼ cup broth, add zucchini, onion, and thyme and then cook for 4 minutes.
2. Pour in remaining broth and water, bring it to a boil, switch heat to the low level, and then simmer for 10 to 15 minutes until tender.
3. Add remaining Ingredients:, stir until mixed, and then continue cooking for 10 minutes or more until cooked.

Nutrition: 184.5 Calories; 0.3 g Fats; 6.8 g Protein; 31 g Carbohydrates; 6 g Fiber;

36. Healthy Alkaline Green Soup

Preparation Time: 10 minutes
Cooking Time: 10 minutes
Servings: 2
Ingredients:
- 2 cups leafy greens
- 1 small zucchini, sliced

- 1 small white onion, peeled, sliced
- 1 medium green bell pepper, cored, sliced
- 2 ½ cups spring water
- Extra:
- ¾ teaspoon salt
- ¼ teaspoon cayenne pepper
- 1 teaspoon dried basil

Directions:
1. Take a medium pot, place it over medium heat, add all the Ingredients:, stir until mixed, and then cook for 5 to 10 minutes until the vegetables turn tender-crisp.
2. Remove pot from heat, puree the soup by using an immersion blender and then serve.

Nutrition: 129 Calories; 0.2 g Fats; 1.1 g Protein; 28 g Carbohydrates; 4.5 g Fiber;

37. Kamut Squash Soup

Preparation Time: 5 minutes
Cooking Time: 32 minutes
Servings: 2
Ingredients:
- 6 tablespoons Kamut berries
- 1 cup chopped white onion
- ½ cup chopped squash
- ½ cup cooked chickpeas
- 1 cup vegetable broth, homemade
- Extra:
- ¼ teaspoon cayenne pepper
- ½ tablespoon chopped tarragon
- 1 bay leaf
- 1 teaspoon chopped thyme
- 1 tablespoon olive oil
- 1 cup spring water, boiling

Directions:
1. Place Kamut in a small bowl, pour in the boiling water, and let it stand for 30 minutes.
2. Then take a medium pot, place it over medium heat, add oil and when hot, add onion, stir in thyme and tarragon and then cook for 5 minutes until tender.
3. Drain Kamut, add to the pot, add bay leaves, pour in the vegetable broth, and then bring it to boil.
4. Cover the pot with its lid, simmer for 20 to 30 minutes, then stir in cayenne pepper and cook for 5 minutes.
5. Remove bay leaf, add chickpeas, and then cook for 2 minutes.

Nutrition: 348.8 Calories; 8.8 g Fats; 11.3 g Protein; 57.2 g

Carbohydrates; 7.8 g Fiber;

38. Creamy Mushroom Soup

Preparation Time: 5 minutes
Cooking Time: 20 minutes
Ingredients:
- 2 cups baby Bella mushrooms, diced
- ½ cup diced red onions
- 1 cup vegetable broth
- 1 ½ cups soft-jelly coconut milk
- Extra:
- ½ teaspoon of sea salt
- ¼ teaspoon cayenne pepper
- 2 teaspoons grapeseed oil

Directions:
1. Take a medium saucepan, place it over medium-high heat, add oil and when hot, add onion, mushrooms, season with salt and pepper, and then cook for 3 to 4 minutes until vegetables turn tender.
2. Then add soy sauce, pour in milk and broth, stir until mixed and bring it to a boil.
3. Switch heat to medium-low level and then simmer the soup for 15 minutes until thickened to the desired level.

Nutrition: 100 Calories; 2 g Fats; 2 g Protein; 18 g Carbohydrates; 2 g Fiber;

39. Onion Soup

Preparation Time: 5 minutes
Cooking Time: 35 minutes
Servings: 2
Ingredients:
- 2 large white onions, peeled, sliced
- ½ cup cubed squash
- 1 sprig of thyme
- 1 tablespoon grapeseed oil
- 2 cups spring water
- Extra:
- ½ teaspoon salt
- ¼ teaspoon cayenne pepper

Directions:
1. Take a medium pot, place it over medium heat, add oil and when hot, add onion and cook for 10 minutes.
2. Add thyme sprig, switch heat to the low level and then cook onions for 15 to 20 minutes until soft, covering the pan with its lid.

3. Add remaining Ingredients:, stir until mixed and simmer for 5 minutes.
4. Ladle soup into bowls and then serve.

Nutrition: 76 Calories; 2.1 g Fats; 2.3 g Protein; 13.1 g Carbohydrates; 2.5 g Fiber;

40. Tomato Soup

Preparation Time: 15 minutes
Cooking Time: 15 minutes
Ingredients:
- 2 teaspoons avocado oil
- 1 medium white onion, chopped
- 3 garlic cloves, minced
- 7 cups fresh plum tomatoes, chopped
- ½ cup fresh sweet basil, chopped
- Sea salt, as needed
- ¼ teaspoon cayenne powder

Directions:
1. In a pan, heat the oil over medium heat and sauté the onion and garlic for about 5–6 minutes.
2. Add the tomatoes and cook for about 6–8 minutes, crushing with the back of spoon occasionally.
3. Stir in the basil, salt, and cayenne powder and remove from the heat.
4. With a hand blender, puree the soup mixture until smooth.
5. Serve immediately.

Nutrition: Calories 75, Fats 0.2 g, Cholesterol 0 mg, Carbohydrates 15.8 g, Fiber 4.6 g, Protein 3.5 g

41. Mushroom Soup

Preparation Time: 15 minutes
Cooking Time: 25 minutes
Servings: 4
Ingredients:
- 2 teaspoons avocado oil
- 1¼ cups fresh Portobello mushrooms, sliced
- 1¼ cups fresh button mushrooms, sliced
- ½ cup white onion, chopped
- 1 garlic clove, crushed
- ½ teaspoon dried thyme
- Sea salt and cayenne powder, as needed
- 1¾ cups unsweetened coconut milk
- 1½ cups spring water

Directions:
1. In a soup pan, heat the avocado oil over medium-high heat and cook the mushrooms, onions, garlic,

thyme, salt, and black pepper for about 5–6 minutes.
2. Add in the coconut milk and water and bring to a boil.
3. Now, adjust the heat to medium-low and simmer for about 10–15 minutes, stirring occasionally.
4. Serve hot.

Nutrition: Calories 177, Fats 13.2 g, Cholesterol 0 mg, Carbohydrates 5.9 g, Fiber 0.9 g, Protein 2.9 g

42. Mixed Greens Soup

Preparation Time: 15 minutes
Cooking Time: 5 minutes
Servings: 3
Ingredients:
- 2 cups fresh kale, tough ribs removed and chopped
- 2 cups fresh watercress
- 2 cups dandelion greens
- 2 garlic cloves, peeled
- 2 cups spring water
- 1 cup unsweetened coconut milk
- 1 tablespoon fresh key lime juice
- ½ teaspoon cayenne powder
- Sea salt, as needed

Directions:
1. Place all soup Ingredients: in a high-powered blender and pulse on high speed until smooth.
2. Transfer the soup into a pan over medium heat and cook for about 3–5 minutes or until heated through.
3. Serve hot.

Nutrition: Calories 168, Fats 10.1 g, Cholesterol 0 mg, Carbohydrates 11 g, Fiber 2.4 g, Protein 4.2 g

43. Squash & Apple Soup

Preparation Time: 15 minutes
Cooking Time: 45 minutes
Servings: 4
Ingredients:
- 2 tablespoon avocado oil
- 1 cup white onion, chopped
- 2 garlic cloves, minced
- 1 teaspoon dried thyme
- 3 cups butternut squash, peeled and cubed
- 2 apples, cored and chopped
- 4 cups spring water
- Sea salt, as needed

Directions:
1. In a soup pan, heat avocado oil over medium heat and sauté the onion for about 5 minutes.
2. Add the garlic and thyme and sauté for about 1 minute.
3. Add the squash and apple and ginger and cook for about 1–2 minutes.
4. Stir in the water and bring to a boil.
5. Now, adjust the heat to low and simmer covered for about 30 minutes.
6. Stir in the salt and remove from the heat.
7. With a hand blender, puree the soup mixture until smooth.
8. Serve immediately.

Nutrition: Calories 129, Fats 0.2 g, Cholesterol 0 mg, Carbohydrates 31.4 g, Fiber 5.9 g, Protein 1.9 g

44. Chickpeas & Squash Stew

Preparation Time: 15 minutes
Cooking Time: 1¼ hours
Servings: 4

Ingredients:
- 2 tablespoons avocado oil
- 1 large white onion, chopped
- 4 garlic cloves, minced
- ½ tablespoon cayenne powder
- 4 large plum tomatoes, seeded and chopped finely
- 1 pound butternut squash; peeled, seeded, and chopped
- 1½ cups spring water
- 1 cup cooked chickpeas
- 2 tablespoons fresh key lime juice
- Sea salt, as needed
- 2 tablespoons fresh parsley, chopped

Directions:
1. In a soup pan, heat the avocado oil over medium heat and sauté the onion for about 4–6 minutes.
2. Add the garlic and cayenne powder and sauté for about 1 minute.
3. Add the tomatoes and cook for about 2–3 minutes.
4. Add the squash and water and bring to a boil.
5. Now, adjust the heat to low and simmer, covered for about 50 minutes.
6. Add the chickpeas and cook for about 10 minutes.
7. Stir in lime juice and salt and remove from heat.
8. Serve hot with the garnishing of parsley.

Nutrition: Calories 150, Fats 0.3 g, Cholesterol 0 mg, Carbohydrates 21.5 g, Protein 5.2 g

45. Chickpeas & Kale Stew

Preparation Time: 15 minutes
Cooking Time: 30 minutes
Servings: 4

Ingredients:
- 1 tablespoon avocado oil
- 1 large onion, chopped
- 2 garlic cloves, minced
- 3 cups cherry tomatoes, chopped finely
- 2 cups spring water
- 2 cups cooked chickpeas
- 2 cups fresh kale, tough ribs removed and chopped
- 1 tablespoon fresh key lime juice
- Sea salt, as needed
- ¼ teaspoon cayenne powder

Directions:
1. In a soup pan, heat avocado oil over medium heat and sauté the onion for about 6 minutes.
2. Stir in the garlic and sauté for about 1 minute.
3. Add the tomatoes and cook for about 2–3 minutes.
4. Add the water and bring to a boil.
5. Now, adjust the heat to low and simmer for about 10 minutes.
6. Stir in the chickpeas and simmer for about 5 minutes.
7. Stir in the spinach and simmer for 3–4 minutes more.
8. Stir in the lime juice and seasoning and remove from the heat.
9. Serve hot.

Nutrition: Calories 206, Fats 0.3 g, Cholesterol 0 mg, Carbohydrates 40.1 g, Fiber 8.4 g, Protein 8.7 g

46. Chickpeas & Veggie Stew

Preparation Time: 20 minutes
Cooking Time: 1 hour 5 minutes
Servings: 6

Ingredients:
- 3 cups portabella mushrooms, chopped
- 4 cups spring water
- 1 cup cooked chickpeas
- 1 cup fresh kale, tough ribs removed and chopped
- 1 cup white onion, chopped
- 1 cup green bell peppers, seeded and chopped
- ½ cup butternut squash; peeled, seeded, and chopped
- 2 plum tomatoes, chopped

- 2 tablespoons grapeseed oil
- 1 teaspoon dried oregano
- 1 teaspoon dried basil
- ½ teaspoon dried thyme
- 2 teaspoons onion powder
- 1 teaspoon cayenne powder
- ½ teaspoon ginger powder
- Sea salt, as needed

Directions:
1. In a soup pan, add all Ingredients: over high heat and bring to a rolling boil.
2. Now, adjust the heat to low and simmer, covered for about 1 hour, stirring occasionally.
3. Serve hot.

Nutrition: Calories 201, Fats 0.7 g, Cholesterol 0 mg, Carbohydrates 28.6 g, Fiber 7.6 g, Protein 8.8 g

47.   Quinoa & Veggie Stew

Preparation Time: 15 minutes
Cooking Time: 1 hour
Servings: 4
Ingredients:
- 2 tablespoons grapeseed oil
- 1 large onion, chopped
- Sea salt, as needed
- 2 cups butternut squash, peeled and cubed
- 3 garlic cloves, minced
- 1 teaspoon ground cumin
- 1 teaspoon cayenne powder
- 2½ cups plum tomatoes, chopped finely
- ½ cup dry quinoa, rinsed
- 3 cups spring water
- 3 cups fresh kale, tough ribs removed and chopped
- 1 tablespoon fresh key lime juice

Directions:
1. In a soup pan, heat the grapeseed oil over medium heat and cook the onion with few pinches of salt for about 4–5 minutes, stirring occasionally.
2. Add the butternut squash and cook for about 3–4 minutes.
3. Stir in the garlic and spices and cook for about 1 minute.
4. Stir in the tomatoes, quinoa, and water and bring to a boil.
5. Now, adjust the heat to low and simmer, covered for about 35 minutes.
6. Stir in the kale and cook for about 10 minutes.

Nutrition: Calories 237, Fats 0.9 g, Cholesterol 0 mg,

Carbohydrates 36.2 g, Fiber 6 g, Protein 6.9 g

48.   Mango & Apple Sauce

Preparation Time: 10 minutes
Cooking Time: 10 minutes
Servings: 6
Ingredients:
- 1 cup mango; peeled, pitted, and chopped
- 2 large apples; peeled, cored, and chopped
- 3–4 tablespoons fresh key lime juice
- 2 tablespoons agave nectar
- ½ cup fresh orange juice

Directions:
1. Add all the sauce Ingredients: in a high-powered blender and pulse on high speed until smooth.
2. Serve immediately.

Nutrition: Calories 85, Fats 0 g, Cholesterol 0 mg, Carbohydrates 22 g, Fiber 2.6 g, Protein 0.6 g

49.   Creamy Squash Soup

Preparation Time: 5 minutes
Cooking Time: 25 minutes
Ingredients:
- ½ of medium white onion, peeled, cubed
- 2 cups cubed squash
- ¼ cup basil leaves
- ½ cup soft-jelly coconut cream
- Extra:
- 1/8 teaspoon sea salt
- 1/8 teaspoon cayenne pepper
- 1 tablespoon grapeseed oil
- 1 cup vegetable broth, homemade

Directions:
1. Take a medium saucepan, place it over medium heat, add oil and when hot, add onion, and then cook for 5 minutes or until softened.
2. Add squash, cook for 10 minutes until golden and begin to soften, pour in the vegetable broth, season with salt and pepper and then bring the soup to boil.
3. Switch heat to medium level and then simmer the soup for 10 minutes until squash turns very soft.
4. Remove pan from heat, puree it by using a stick blender until smooth, and then garnish with basil.

Nutrition: 183 Calories; 14.4 g Fats; 1.9 g Protein; 13.4 g Carbohydrates; 2.7 g Fiber;

50.   Healing Ginger Carrot Soup

Preparation Time: 10 minutes
Cooking Time: 15 minutes
Servings: 2

Ingredients:

- 1 tablespoon fresh ginger
- Sea salt and pepper- to taste
- 2 garlic cloves
- ½ onion- quartered
- 4 carrots- washed and peeled
- 2 cups vegetable stock
- 1 teaspoon turmeric

Directions:

1. Add all your Ingredients: to a huge pot and bring to a boil. Once boiled, let it simmer for an hour. When the carrots are soft, blend using an immersion blender until smooth.
2. Garnish with some hemp seeds on top if desired.

Nutrition: Calories 443, Fat 8g, Fiber1g, Carbohydrates 8g, Protein 3g

51. Creamy Broccoli Soup

Preparation Time: 5 minutes
Cooking Time: 10 minutes
Servings: 5

Ingredients:

- 2 cups vegetable stock
- 4 cups broccoli, chopped
- 1 red pepper, chopped
- 1 avocado
- 2 onions, chopped
- 2 celery stalks, sliced
- Ginger to taste
- 1 tablespoon salt

Directions:

1. Warm vegetable stock in a small pot. Add broccoli and season with salt to taste. Simmer for 5 minutes.
2. Add the broccoli in a blender with pepper, avocado, onions, and celery stalks. Add some water for thinning then blend until smooth.
3. Serve when warm with ginger to your liking. Garnish with a lemon slice. Enjoy.

Nutrition: Calories: 270, Fat: 18g, Carbohydrates: 17g, Protein: 12g, Fiber: 3.5g

VEGETABLES

52. Power Pesto Zoodles

Preparation Time: 10 minutes
Cooking Time: 5 minutes
Ingredients:

- 2 zucchini
- 1 avocado, peeled, pitted
- ½ cup cherry tomatoes
- 2 tablespoons walnuts
- ½ of key lime, juiced
- Extra:
- ¼ teaspoon salt
- 1/8 teaspoon cayenne pepper
- 2 teaspoons grapeseed oil
- 2 tablespoons olive oil

Directions:

1. Prepare the zucchini noodles and for this, cut them into thin strips by using a vegetable peeler or use a spiralizer.
2. Then take a medium skillet pan, add oil in it and when hot, add zucchini noodles in it and then cook for 3 to 5 minutes until tender-crisp.
3. Meanwhile, place the remaining Ingredients: in a food processor and then pulse until the creamy paste comes together.
4. When zucchini noodles have sautéed, drain and place them in a large bowl and add the blended sauce in it.
5. Add 2 tablespoons of water and then toss until well combined.
6. Garnish the zoodles with grated coconut and then serve.

Nutrition: 214 Calories; 1017.10 g Fats; 4.8 g Protein; 13.2 g Carbohydrates; 6.1 g Fiber;

53. Spinach With Chickpeas and Lemon

Preparation Time: 5 minute
Cooking Time: 10 minutes
Servings: 2
Ingredients:

- 3 tablespoons oil
- 1 onion, thinly sliced
- 4 garlic cloves, minced
- 1 tablespoons ginger, grated
- 1/2 container cherry tomatoes
- 1 lemon, freshly zested and juiced
- 1 tablespoon red pepper flakes, crushed
- 1 can chickpeas
- Salt to taste

Directions:

1. Add oil in a skillet and cook onions until browned. Add garlic cloves, ginger, tomatoes, zest, and pepper flakes. Cook for 4 minutes.
2. Add chickpeas and cook for 3 more minutes. Add spinach and cook until they start to wilt.
3. Add lemon juice and season with salt to taste. Cook for 2 more minutes.
4. Serve and enjoy.

Nutrition: Calories: 209 Fat: 8.1g Total Carbohydrates: 28.5g Protein: 22.5g Fiber: 6g

54. Mushroom Sauce

Preparation Time: 5 minutes;
Cooking Time: 12 minutes
Ingredients:

- ¾ tablespoon spelt flour
- ¼ of onion, peeled, diced
- 4 ounces sliced mushrooms
- ½ cup walnut milk, homemade
- 1 tablespoon chopped walnuts
- Extra:
- ¼ teaspoon salt
- 1/8 teaspoon cayenne pepper
- ½ teaspoon dried thyme
- 1 tablespoon grapeseed oil
- ¼ cup vegetable broth, homemade

Directions:

1. Take a medium skillet pan, place it over medium heat, add oil and when hot, add onion and mushrooms, season with 1/16 teaspoon each of salt and cayenne pepper, and then cook for 4 minutes until tender.
2. Stir in spelt flour until coated, cook for 1 minute, slowly whisk in milk and vegetable broth and then season with remaining salt and cayenne pepper.
3. Switch heat to low-level, cook for 5 to 7 minutes until sauce has thickened slightly and then stir in walnuts and thyme.
4. Serve straight away with spelt flour bread.

Nutrition: 65.3 Calories; 1.6 g Fats; 3.5 g Protein; 9.6 g Carbohydrates; 1 g Fiber;

55. Vegetable Fajitas

Preparation Time: 10 minutes
Cooking Time: 8 minutes
Ingredients:
- 2 Portobello mushroom caps, 1/3-inch sliced
- ¾ of red bell pepper, sliced
- ½ of onion, peeled, sliced
- ½ of key lime, juiced
- 2 spelt flour tortillas
- Extra:
- 1/3 teaspoon salt
- ¼ teaspoon cayenne pepper
- ¼ teaspoon onion powder
- 1 tablespoon grapeseed oil

Directions:
1. Take a medium skillet pan, place it over medium heat, add oil and when hot, add onion and red pepper, and then cook for 2 minutes until tender-crisp.
2. Add mushrooms slices, sprinkle with all the seasoning, stir until mixed, and then cook for 5 minutes until vegetables turn soft.
3. Heat the tortilla until warm, distribute vegetables in their center, drizzle with lime juice, and then roll tightly.

Nutrition: 337 Calories; 3.7 g Fats; 2.6 g Protein; 73.3 g Carbohydrates; 21.3 g Fiber;

56. Chickpea and Mushroom Curry

Preparation Time: 5 minutes
Cooking Time: 12 minutes
Ingredients:
- 1 cup cooked chickpea

- 1 small white onion, peeled, diced
- ½ of medium green bell pepper, cored, chopped
- 1 cup diced mushrooms
- 8 cherry tomatoes, chopped
- Extra:
- ½ teaspoon salt
- ¼ teaspoon cayenne pepper
- 1 teaspoon grapeseed oil

Directions:
1. Take a medium skillet pan, place it over medium heat, add oil and when hot, add onion, tomatoes, and bell pepper and then cook for 2 minutes.
2. Add chickpeas and mushrooms, season with and cayenne pepper, stir until combined, and switch heat to medium-low level and then simmer for 10 minutes until cooked, covering the pan with its lid.

Nutrition: 194.7 Calories; 8.5 g Fats; 5.8 g Protein; 25.7 g Carbohydrates; 5.4 g Fiber;

57. Vegetable Low Mein

Preparation Time: 5 minutes
Cooking Time: 10 minutes
Ingredients:
- 2 cups cooked spelt noodles
- ½ of medium green bell pepper, cored, sliced
- ½ of medium red bell pepper, cored, sliced
- 1 medium white onion, cored, sliced
- ½ cup sliced mushrooms
- Extra:
- 2/3 teaspoon salt
- ¼ teaspoon onion powder
- 1/3 teaspoon cayenne pepper
- 1 key lime juiced
- 1 tablespoon sesame oil

Directions:
1. Take a large skillet pan, place it over medium heat, add oil and when hot, add all the vegetables and cook for 3 to 5 minutes until tender-crisp.
2. Add all the spices, drizzle with lime juice, stir until mixed, and then cook for 1 minute.
3. Add noodles, toss until well mixed and then cook for 2 to 3 minutes until hot.

Nutrition: 330 Calories; 11 g Fats; 10 g Protein; 48 g Carbohydrates; 4 g Fiber;

58. Spiced Okra Curry

Preparation Time: 5 minutes
Cooking Time: 10 minutes
Ingredients:

- 1 ½ cup okra
- 8 cherry tomatoes, chopped
- 1 medium onion, peeled, sliced
- ¾ cup vegetable broth, homemade
- Extra:
- 6 teaspoons spice mix
- ¼ teaspoon salt
- ½ tablespoon grapeseed oil
- ¼ teaspoon cayenne pepper
- ¾ cup tomato sauce, alkaline
- 6 tablespoons soft-jelly coconut milk

Directions:

1. Take a large skillet pan, place it over medium heat, add oil and warm, add onion, and then cook for 5 minutes until golden brown.
2. Add spice mix, add remaining Ingredients: into the pan except for okra, stir until mixed, and then bring the mixture to a simmer.
3. Add okra, stir until mixed, and then cook for 10 to 15 minutes over medium-low heat setting until cooked.

Nutrition: 137 Calories; 8.4 g Fats; 4 g Protein; 15 g Carbohydrates; 5.6 g Fiber;

59. Baked Portobello Mushrooms

Preparation Time: 10 minutes
Cooking Time: 30 minutes
Ingredients:

- 2 caps of Portobello mushrooms, destemmed
- 2/3 teaspoon minced onion
- 2/3 teaspoon minced sage
- 2/3 teaspoon thyme
- 2/3 tablespoon key lime juice
- Extra:
- 2 tablespoons alkaline soy sauce

Directions:

1. Switch on the oven, then set it to 400 degrees F and let it preheat.
2. Take a baking dish and then arrange mushroom caps in it, cut side up.
3. Take a small bowl, place remaining Ingredients: in it, stir until mixed, brush the mixture over inside and outside mushrooms, and then let them marinate for 15 minutes.
4. Bake the mushrooms for 30 minutes, flipping halfway, and then serve.

Nutrition: 137 Calories; 8.4 g Fats; 4 g Protein; 15 g Carbohydrates; 5.6 g Fiber;

60. Chard and Lime Pasta

Preparation Time: 5 minutes
Cooking Time: 5 minutes
Ingredients:

- 1 head of Swiss chard, cut into ½-inch pieces
- 1 cup spelt pasta, cooked
- 2 green onions, sliced
- ¼ cup cilantro
- 1 key lime, juiced, zested
- Extra:
- ¼ teaspoon salt
- ¼ teaspoon cayenne pepper
- 1 tablespoon olive oil

Directions:

1. Take a large skillet pan, place it over medium heat, add oil and when hot, add chard pieces and then cook for 4 minutes or more until wilted.
2. Remove pan from heat, transfer chards to a large bowl, add remaining Ingredients: and then toss until combined.

Nutrition: 224 Calories; 7 g Fats; 7 g Protein; 33 g Carbohydrates; 2 g Fiber;

61. Roasted Squash and Apples

Preparation Time: 10 minutes
Cooking Time: 35 minutes
Ingredients:

- 1 ½ pounds butternut squash, peeled, deseeded, cut into chunks
- 2 apples, cored, cut into ½-inch pieces
- 2 tablespoons agave syrup
- 1/2 teaspoon sea salt
- Extra:
- 2 tablespoons grapeseed oil

Directions:

1. Switch on the oven, then set it to 375 degrees F and let it preheat.
2. Meanwhile, take a baking sheet and then spread squash pieces on it.

3. Take a small bowl, pour in oil, stir in salt and allspice until mixed, and then drizzle over squash pieces.
4. Cover the pan with foil and then bake for 20 minutes.
5. Meanwhile, place apple pieces in a medium bowl, drizzle with agave syrup, and then toss until coated.
6. When squash has baked, unwrap the baking sheet, spoon into the bowl containing apple and then stir until mixed.
7. Spread apple-squash mixture evenly on the baking sheet and then continue baking for 15 minutes.

Nutrition: 126.4 Calories; 4.9 g Fats; 1.1 g Protein; 22.2 g Carbohydrates; 5.1 g Fiber;

62. Mushroom Steak

Preparation Time: 10 minutes
Cooking Time: 10 minutes
Ingredients:
- 2 portabella mushroom caps, 1/8-inch thick sliced
- ½ cup sliced green bell peppers
- ½ cup sliced white onions
- ½ cup sliced red bell peppers
- ¼ cup alkaline sauce
- Extra:
- ½ teaspoon of sea salt
- ½ tablespoon onion powder
- ½ teaspoon dried oregano
- ½ teaspoon dried thyme
- ½ tablespoon grapeseed oil
- 2 spelt flatbread, toasted

Directions:
1. Take a medium bowl, place sauce in it, add all the seasoning, and then whisk until combined.
2. Add mushroom slices, toss until coated, and then let them marinate for a minimum of 30 minutes, tossing halfway.
3. Then take a pan, place it over medium-high heat, add oil and when hot, add onion and pepper and cook for 3 to 5 minutes until tender-crisp.
4. Add mushroom slices, stir until mixed and continue cooking for 5 minutes.
5. Distribute vegetables evenly between flatbread, roll them, and then serve.

Nutrition: 302 Calories; 18 g Fats; 2 g Protein; 27 g Carbohydrates; 3 g Fiber;

63. Chayote Mushroom Stew

Preparation Time: 10 minutes
Cooking Time: 40 minutes
Ingredients:
- 2/3 cup chayote squash cubes
- 1 cups sliced mushrooms
- 1/3 cup diced white onions
- ½ cup chickpea flour
- 1/3 cup vegetable broth, homemade
- Extra:
- 1/3 tablespoon onion powder
- 2/3 teaspoon sea salt
- 2/3 teaspoon dried basil
- 1/3 teaspoon crushed red pepper
- 2 cups spring water
- ½ tablespoon grapeseed oil
- 1/3 cup hemp milk, homemade

Directions:
1. Take a medium pot, place it over medium-high heat, add oil and when hot, add onion and mushroom, and then cook for 5 minutes.
2. Switch heat to medium level, pour in 1 cup water, milk, and broth, add chayote and all the seasoning, stir until mixed, and then bring it to a simmer, covering the pan with lid.
3. Pour remaining water into a food processor, add chickpea flour, pulse until blended, add to the pot and then stir until mixed.
4. Switch heat to the low level, simmer for 30 minutes, and then serve.

Nutrition: 173 Calories; 9 g Fats; 2 g Protein; 20 g Carbohydrates; 2 g Fiber;

64. Veggie Lettuce Wraps

Preparation Time: 10 minutes
Cooking Time: 0 minutes
Ingredients:
- ½ cup cherry tomatoes, halved
- 1 avocado, peeled, pitted, sliced
- ½ cup sprouts
- ½ of medium white onion, peeled, sliced
- 2 large lettuce leaves
- Extra:
- 2 tablespoons key lime juice
- ½ tablespoon raisins
- ¼ teaspoon salt
- 1/8 teaspoon cayenne pepper

Directions:
1. Take a small bowl, add lime juice, add salt and pepper and then stir until mixed.
2. Take a medium bowl, place all the vegetables in it except for lettuce, drizzle with the lime juice mixture and then toss until mixed.
3. Place a lettuce leaves on a plate, top with half of the vegetable mixture, and then roll it tightly.
4. Repeat with the other lettuce wrap and then serve.

Nutrition: 155 Calories; 10.5 g Fats; 4.8 g Protein; 13.2 g Carbohydrates; 3.5 g Fiber;

65. Zucchini Linguine

Preparation Time: 10 minutes
Cooking Time: 8 minutes
Ingredients:
- 2 zucchini, spiralized
- ½ cup sliced mushrooms
- ½ teaspoon dried thyme
- ½ cup alkaline Avocado sauce
- ¼ cup chopped cilantro
- Extra:
- 1/3 teaspoon salt
- 1/8 teaspoon cayenne pepper
- 1 tablespoon grapeseed oil
- ½ teaspoon dried oregano

Directions:
1. Take a skillet pan, place it over medium heat, add oil and when hot, add mushrooms and cilantro and then cook for 3 to 5 minutes until tender.
2. Add avocado sauce, season with salt, pepper, oregano, and thyme, stir until mixed and cook for 1 to 2 minutes until warmed.
3. Place zucchini noodles in a large bowl, drizzle with some oil, and then toss until well coated.
4. Add avocado mixture, toss until combined, and then serve.

Nutrition: 284 Calories; 23.6 g Fats; 5.7 g Protein; 18.8 g Carbohydrates; 9.7 g Fiber;

66. Spiced Mushroom Bowl

Preparation Time: 5 minutes
Cooking Time: 10 minutes
Ingredients:
- 1 ½ cup sliced mushrooms
- 8 cherry tomatoes, chopped
- 1 medium onion, peeled, sliced
- ¾ cup vegetable broth, homemade

- Extra:
- 6 teaspoons spice mix
- ¼ teaspoon salt
- ½ tablespoon grapeseed oil
- ¼ teaspoon cayenne pepper
- ¾ cup tomato sauce, alkaline
- 6 tablespoons soft-jelly coconut milk

Directions:
1. Take a large skillet pan, place it over medium heat, add oil and warm, add onion, and then cook for 5 minutes until golden brown.
2. Add spice mix, add remaining Ingredients: into the pan except for okra, stir until mixed, and then bring the mixture to a simmer.
3. Add mushrooms, stir until mixed, and then cook for 10 to 15 minutes over medium-low heat setting until cooked.

Nutrition: 186 Calories; 3.4 g Fats; 2.1 g Protein; 36.7 g Carbohydrates; 3.5 g Fiber;

67. Chickpea and Kale Curry

Preparation Time: 5 minutes
Cooking Time: 10 minutes
Ingredients:
- 2 cups cooked chickpeas
- 2/3 teaspoon salt
- 1 cup Kale leaves
- 2/3 cup soft-jelly coconut cream
- 2 tablespoons grapeseed oil
- Extra:
- 1/3 teaspoon cayenne pepper

Directions:
1. Switch on the oven, then set it to 425 degrees F and let it preheat.
2. Then take a medium baking sheet, spread chickpeas on it, drizzle with 1 tablespoon oil, sprinkle with all the seasonings and then bake for 15 minutes until roasted.
3. Then take a frying pan, place it over medium heat, add remaining oil and when hot, add kale and cook for 5 minutes.
4. Add roasted chickpeas, pour in the cream, stir until mixed and then simmer for 4 minutes, squashing chickpeas slightly.

Nutrition: 522 Calories; 38 g Fats; 15 g Protein; 26 g Carbohydrates; 8 g Fiber;

68.   Hummus Wrap

Preparation Time: 10 minutes
Cooking Time: 8 minutes

Ingredients

- ½ cup iceberg lettuce
- 1 zucchini, sliced
- 2 cherry tomatoes, sliced
- 2 spelt flour tortillas
- 4 tablespoons homemade hummus
- Extra:
- ¼ teaspoon salt
- 1/8 teaspoon cayenne pepper
- 1 tablespoon grapeseed oil

Directions

1. Take a grill pan, grease it oil and let it preheat over medium-high heat setting.
2. Meanwhile, place zucchini slices in a large bowl, sprinkle with salt and cayenne pepper, drizzle with oil and then toss until coated.
3. Arrange zucchini slices on the grill pan and then cook for 2 to 3 minutes per side until developed grill marks.
4. Assemble tortillas and for this, heat the tortilla on the grill pan until warm and develop grill marks and spread 2 tablespoons of hummus over each tortilla.
5. Distribute grilled zucchini slices over the tortillas, top with lettuce and tomato slices, and then wrap tightly.
6. Storage instructions:
7. Cover each wrap with a plastic wrap and foil and then refrigerate for up to 5 days.
8. Reheating instructions:
9. When ready to eat, bring the wrap to room temperature or reheat in the oven for 1 to 2 minutes until hot and then serve.

Nutrition: 264.5 Calories; 5.1 g Fats; 8.5 g Protein; 34.5 g Carbohydrates; 5 g Fiber;

69.   Tomato Sauce

Preparation Time: 15 minutes
Cooking Time: 50 minutes
Servings: 24

Ingredients:

- 18 plum tomatoes, halved
- ½ of red bell pepper, seeded and halved
- ½ of red onion, halved
- ½ of sweet onion, halved
- 1 medium shallot, halved

- 2 tablespoons grapeseed oil
- 3 teaspoons dried basil, divided
- 3 teaspoons sea salt
- 1 tablespoon agave nectar
- 2 teaspoons dried oregano
- 2 teaspoons onion powder
- 1/8 teaspoon cayenne powder

Directions:

1. Preheat your oven to 400°F.
2. Line a baking sheet with parchment paper.
3. In a bowl, add tomatoes, bell pepper, onions, shallot, oil, 1 teaspoon of basil, and 1 teaspoon of salt and toss to coat well.
4. Arrange the vegetables onto the prepared baking sheet, cut-side down.
5. Roast for about 30 minutes, flipping the vegetables once halfway through.
6. Remove the baking sheet from oven and set aside to cool slightly.
7. In a high-powered blender, add the roasted vegetables and pulse on high speed until smooth.
8. In a pan, add the pureed vegetables and remaining Ingredients: over low heat and simmer for about 20 minutes.
9. Remove from the heat and set aside to cool completely before serving.

Nutrition: Calories 33 Fats 0.1 g Cholesterol 0 mg Carbohydrates 5.3 g Fiber .4 g Protein 0.9 g

70.   Lettuce Wraps

Preparation Time: 15 minutes
Cooking Time: 15 minutes
Servings: 3

Ingredients:

- ¾ cup fresh kale, tough ribs removed and torn
- 1 cup cucumber, sliced
- 1 cup cherry tomatoes, halved
- Sea salt, as needed
- 6 large lettuce leaves

Directions:

1. In a large bowl, add the kale, cucumber, tomato, and salt and mix well.
2. Arrange the lettuce leaves onto serving plates.
3. Divide the kale mixture onto each lettuce leaf evenly.
4. Serve immediately.

Nutrition: Calories 26 Fats 0 g Cholesterol 0 mg Carbohydrates 5.4 g Fiber 1.2 g Protein 1.3 g

71. Veggies Burgers

Preparation Time: 15 minutes
Cooking Time: 20 minutes
Servings: 4
Ingredients:

- ½ cup fresh kale, tough ribs removed and chopped
- ½ cup green bell peppers, seeded and chopped
- ½ cup onions, chopped
- 1 plum tomato, chopped
- 2 teaspoons fresh oregano, chopped
- 2 teaspoons fresh basil, chopped
- 1 teaspoon dried dill
- 1 teaspoon onion powder
- ½ teaspoon ginger powder
- ½ teaspoon cayenne powder
- Sea salt, as needed
- 1 cup chickpeas flour
- ¼–½ cup spring water
- 2 tablespoons grapeseed oil
- 4 cups fresh arugula

Directions:

1. In a bowl, add all vegetables, herbs, spices, and salt and mix well.
2. Add the flour and mix well.
3. Slowly, add the water and mix until a thick mixture is formed.
4. Make desired-sized patties from the mixture.
5. In a skillet, heat the grapeseed oil over medium-high heat and cook the patties for about 2–3 minutes per side.
6. Divide the arugula onto serving plates and top each with 2 burgers.
7. Serve immediately.

Nutrition: Calories 177 Fats 0.9 g Cholesterol 0 mg Carbohydrates 19.2 g Fiber 4.1g Protein 6.6 g

72. Veggie Balls in Tomato Sauce

Preparation Time: 20 minutes
Cooking Time: 15 minutes
Servings: 8
Ingredients:

- 1½ cups cooked chickpeas
- 2 cups fresh button mushrooms
- ½ cup onions, chopped
- ¼ cup green bell peppers, seeded and chopped
- 2 teaspoons oregano
- 2 teaspoons fresh basil

- 1 teaspoon savory
- 1 teaspoon dried sage
- 1 teaspoon dried dill
- 1 tablespoon onion powder
- ½ teaspoon cayenne powder
- ½ teaspoon ginger powder
- Sea salt, as needed
- ½–1 cup chickpea flour
- 6 cups homemade tomato sauce
- 2 tablespoons grapeseed oil

Directions:

1. In a food processor, add the chickpeas, veggies, herbs, and spices and pulse until well combined.
2. Transfer the mixture into a large bowl with flour and mix until well combined.
3. Make desired-sized balls from the mixture.
4. In a skillet, heat the grapeseed oil over medium-high heat and cook the balls in 2 batches for about 4–5 minutes or until golden-brown from all sides.
5. In a large pan, add the tomato sauce and veggie balls over medium heat and simmer for about 5 minutes.
6. Serve hot.

Nutrition: Calories 247 Fats 0.7 g Cholesterol 0 mg Carbohydrates 38.8 g Fiber 10.7 g Protein 11.8 g

73. Veggie Kabobs

Preparation Time: 20 minutes
Cooking Time: 10 minutes
Servings: 4
Ingredients:

- Marinade
- 2 garlic cloves, minced
- 2 teaspoons fresh basil, minced
- 2 teaspoons fresh oregano, minced
- ½ teaspoon cayenne powder
- Sea salt, as needed
- 2 tablespoons fresh key lime juice
- 2 tablespoons avocado oil
- Veggies
- 2 large zucchinis, cut into thick slices
- 8 large button mushrooms, quartered
- 2 red bell pepper, seeded and cubed
- 1 large onion, cubed

Directions:

1. For marinade: In a bowl, add all Ingredients: and mix until well combined.
2. Add the vegetables and toss to coat well.

3. Cover and refrigerate to marinate for at least 6–8 hours.
4. Preheat the grill to medium-high heat. Generously, grease the grill grate.
5. Remove the vegetables from the bowl and thread onto pre-soaked wooden skewers.
6. Place the veggie skewers onto the preheated grill and cook for about 8–10 minutes or until done completely, flipping occasionally.
7. Serve hot.

Nutrition: Calories 85 Fats 0.3 g Cholesterol 0 mg Carbohydrates 16.4 g Fiber 4.6 g Protein 4.7 g

74.   Spiced Okra

Preparation Time: 10 minutes
Cooking Time: 13 minutes
Servings: 2
Ingredients:
- 1 tablespoon avocado oil
- ¾ pound okra pods, trimmed and cut into 2-inch pieces
- ½ teaspoon ground cumin
- ½ teaspoon cayenne powder
- Sea salt, as needed

Directions:
1. In a skillet, heat the avocado oil over medium heat and stir-fry the okra for about 2 minutes.
2. Now, adjust the heat to low and cook covered for about 6–8 minutes, stirring occasionally.
3. Add the cumin, cayenne powder, and salt and stir to combine.
4. Now, adjust the heat to medium and cook uncovered for about 2–3 minutes more.
5. Remove from the heat and serve hot.

Nutrition: Calories 81 Fats 0.3 g Cholesterol 0 mg Carbohydrates 13.5 g Fiber 5.9 g Protein 3.5 g

75.   Mushroom Curry

Preparation Time: 15 minutes
Cooking Time: 25 minutes
Servings: 4
Ingredients:
- 2 cups plum tomatoes, chopped
- 2 tablespoons grapeseed oil
- 1 small onion, chopped finely
- ¼ teaspoon cayenne powder
- 4 cups fresh button mushrooms, sliced
- 1¼ cups spring water

- ¼ cup unsweetened coconut milk
- Sea salt, as needed

Directions:
1. In a food processor, add the tomatoes and pulse until smooth paste forms.
2. In a pan, heat the oil over medium heat and sauté the onion for about 5–6 minutes.
3. Add the tomato paste and cook for about 5 minutes.
4. Stir in the mushrooms, water, and coconut milk and bring to a boil.
5. Cook for about 10–12 minutes, stirring occasionally.
6. Season with the salt and remove from the heat.
7. Serve hot.

Nutrition: Calories 133 Fats 3.9 g Cholesterol 0 mg Carbohydrates 8.3 g Fiber 2.5 g Protein 3.5 g

76.   Mushrooms with Bell Peppers

Preparation Time: 15 minutes
Cooking Time: 10 minutes
Servings: 4
Ingredients:
- 1 tablespoon grapeseed oil
- 3 cups fresh button mushrooms, sliced
- ¾ cup red bell peppers, seeded and cut into long strips
- ¾ cup yellow bell peppers, seeded and cut into long strips
- 1½ cup white onions, cut into long strips
- 2 teaspoons fresh sweet basil
- 2 teaspoons fresh oregano
- ½ teaspoon cayenne powder
- Sea salt, as needed

Directions:
1. In a skillet, heat the grapeseed oil over medium-high heat and sauté the mushrooms, bell peppers, and onion for about 5–6 minutes.
2. Add in the herbs, cayenne pepper, and salt and cook for about 2–3 minutes.
3. Add in the lime juice and remove the skillet of veggies from heat.
4. Serve hot.

Nutrition: Calories 76 Fats 0.4 g Cholesterol 0 mg Carbohydrates 8.8 g Protein 2.7 g

77.   Pepper & Tomato Bake

Preparation Time: 15 minutes

Cooking Time: 35 minutes
Servings: 6
Ingredients:
- Herb Sauce
- 4 garlic cloves, chopped
- ½ cup fresh parsley, chopped
- ½ cup fresh basil, chopped
- 3 tablespoons avocado oil
- 2 tablespoons fresh key lime juice
- ½ teaspoon ground cumin
- ½ teaspoon cayenne powder
- Sea salt, as needed
- Veggies
- 2 large red bell peppers, seeded and sliced
- 2 large yellow bell peppers, seeded and sliced
- 1 pound plum tomatoes, cut into 8 wedges
- 2 tablespoons avocado oil

Directions:
1. Preheat your oven to 350°F.
2. Lightly grease a large shallow baking dish.
3. For sauce: Add all Ingredients: in a food processor and pulse on high speed until smooth.
4. In a large bowl, add the bell peppers, sauce, and herb sauce and gently toss to coat.
5. Place the bell pepper mixture into the prepared baking dish and drizzle with oil.
6. With a large piece of foil, cover the baking dish.
7. Bake for approximately 35 minutes.
8. Uncover the baking dish and bake for approximately 20–30 minutes more.
9. Serve hot.

Nutrition: Calories 61 Fats 0.3 g Cholesterol 0 mg Carbohydrates 10.8 g Fiber 2.8 g Protein 2 g

78. **Zucchini with Tomatoes**

Preparation Time: 15 minutes
Cooking Time: 18 minutes
Cooking Time: 33 minutes
Servings: 2
Ingredients:
- 1 tablespoon avocado oil
- 2 garlic cloves, minced
- ¼ teaspoon dried oregano, crushed
- 2 cups cherry tomatoes, halved
- 1 cup onion, chopped
- 4 cups zucchinis, sliced
- Sea salt, as needed
- 1 teaspoon fresh key lime juice

Directions:
1. In a skillet, heat avocado oil over medium heat and sauté onion for about 4–5 minutes.
2. Add garlic, green chili, oregano, and cumin and sauté for about 1 minute.
3. Add zucchini and cook for about 3–4 minutes.
4. Add tomatoes and salt and cook for about 7–8 minutes.
5. Stir in lime juice and serve hot.

Nutrition: Calories 106 Fats 0.3 g Cholesterol 0 mg Carbohydrates 21.5 g Fiber 6.3 g Protein 5.2 g

79. **Zucchini Noodles with Tomatoes**

Preparation Time: 15 minutes
Cooking Time: 7 minutes
Servings: 3
Ingredients:
- 2 tablespoons avocado oil
- 2 medium zucchinis, spiralized with Blade C
- 1 garlic clove, minced
- 1 cup cherry tomatoes, sliced
- Sea salt, as needed

Directions:
1. In a skillet, heat avocado oil over medium heat and cook the zucchini for about 3 minutes.
2. Add the garlic and cook for about 1 minute.
3. Add the cherry tomatoes and salt and cook for about 2–3 minutes.
4. Serve hot.

Nutrition: Calories 46 Fats 0.3 g Cholesterol 0 mg Carbohydrates 7.6 g Fiber 2.6 g Protein 2.3 g

80. **Kamut Burgers**

Preparation Time: 20 minutes
Cooking Time: 20 minutes
Servings: 6
Ingredients:
- 3 cups cooked kamut cereal
- 1 cup spelt flour
- ½ cup unsweetened hemp milk
- 1 cup green bell peppers, seeded and chopped
- 1 cup red onions, chopped
- 1 tablespoon fresh oregano, chopped
- 1 tablespoon fresh basil, chopped
- 1 teaspoon onion powder
- 1 teaspoon sea salt

- ½ teaspoon cayenne powder
- 4 tablespoons grapeseed oil
- 8 cups fresh baby kale

Directions:
1. In a bowl, add all the Ingredients: (except for oil and kale) and mix until well combined.
2. Make 12 equal-sized patties from the mixture.
3. In a skillet, heat 2 tablespoons of the grapeseed oil over medium-high heat and cook 6 patties for about 4–5 minutes per side.
4. Repeat with the remaining oil and patties.
5. Divide the kale onto serving plates and top each with 2 burgers.
6. Serve immediately.

Nutrition: Calories 242 Fats 1 g Cholesterol 0 mg Carbohydrates 33.6 g Fiber 5.8 g Protein 7.6 g

81. Chickpeas Falafel with Tzatziki Sauce

Preparation Time: 20 minutes
Cooking Time: 20 minutes
Servings: 6
Ingredients:
- Falafel
- 1 pound dry chickpeas; soaked overnight, drained, and rinsed
- 1 small onion, chopped roughly
- ¼ cup fresh parsley, chopped
- 4 garlic cloves, peeled
- 1½ tablespoons chickpea flour
- Sea salt, as needed
- ½ teaspoon cayenne powder
- ½ cup grapeseed oil
- Tzatziki Sauce
- ½ cup Brazil nuts, soaked in spring water for 6–8 hours
- ½ cup spring water
- ¼ cup cucumber, chopped
- 1 tablespoon fresh key lime juice
- 1 garlic clove, minced
- 1 teaspoon fresh dill
- Pinch of sea salt
- For Serving
- 12 cups fresh lettuce

Directions:
1. For falafel: In a food processor, add all the Ingredients: and pulse until well combined and a coarse meal-like mixture forms.

2. Transfer the falafel mixture into a bowl.
3. With a plastic wrap, cover the bowl of mixture and refrigerate for about 1–2 hours.
4. With 2 tablespoons of the mixture, make balls.
5. In a large skillet, heat the oil to 375°F.
6. Add the falafels in 2 batches and cook for about 5–6 minutes or until golden-brown from all aides.
7. For tzatziki sauce: In a blender, add all the Ingredients: and pulse until smooth.
8. With a slotted spoon, transfer the falafels onto a paper towel-lined plate to drain.
9. Divide the lettuce and falafels onto serving plates evenly.
10. Serve alongside the tzatziki.

Nutrition: Calories 260 19.2 g Fats 1.7 g Cholesterol 0 mg 196 mg Carbohydrates 18.5 g Fiber 4 g 1.5 g Protein 5.7 g

82. Chickpea-Stuffed Avocados

Preparation Time: 15 minutes
Cooking Time: 15 minutes
Servings: 2
Ingredients:
- 1 large avocado, halved and pitted
- ¾ cup cooked chickpeas
- ¼ cup tomato, chopped
- ¼ cup cucumber, chopped
- ¼ cup onion, chopped
- 1 small garlic clove, minced
- 1 tablespoon fresh basil, chopped
- 1½ tablespoons fresh key lime juice
- ½ teaspoon olive oil

Directions:
1. With a small spoon, scoop out the flesh from each avocado half.
2. Then, cut half of the avocado flesh into equal-sized cubes.
3. In a large bowl, add avocado cubes and remaining Ingredients: and toss to coat well.
4. Stuff each avocado half with chickpeas mixture evenly and serve immediately.

Nutrition: Calories 337.1.9 g Fats 4.4 g Cholesterol 0 mg 277 mg Carbohydrates 32.2 g Fiber 4.4 g 1.9 g Protein 7 g

83. Chickpeas Curry

Preparation Time: 15 minutes
Cooking Time: 25 minutes
Servings: 6
Ingredients:

- 3 tablespoons avocado oil
- 1 medium onion, chopped finely
- 2 garlic cloves, minced
- 1 teaspoon ground cumin
- ½ teaspoon cayenne powder
- Sea salt, as needed
- 2 large plum tomatoes, chopped finely
- 3 cups cooked chickpeas
- 2 cups spring water
- ¼ cup fresh parsley, chopped

Directions:

1. In a pan, heat the avocado oil over medium heat and sauté the onion and garlic for about 6–8 minutes.
2. Stir in the spices and salt and cook for about 1–2 minutes.
3. Stir in the tomatoes, chickpeas, and water and bring to a boil over high heat.
4. Now, adjust the heat to medium and simmer for 10–15 minutes or until desired thickness.
5. Serve hot with a garnish of parsley.

Nutrition: Calories 166 Fats 0.4 g Cholesterol 0 mg Carbohydrates 27.7 g Fiber 7.8 g Protein 8.3 g

84.   Chickpeas & Zucchini Chili

Preparation Time: 15 minutes
Cooking Time: 1 hour 10 minutes
Servings: 8
Ingredients:

- 2 tablespoons avocado oil
- 1 medium white onion, chopped
- 1 large red bell pepper, seeded and chopped
- 4 garlic cloves, minced
- 1 teaspoon dried thyme
- 1 tablespoon cayenne powder
- Sea salt, as needed
- 2 medium zucchinis, chopped
- 3 cups plum tomatoes, chopped
- 3 cups cooked chickpeas
- 2 cups spring water

Directions:

1. In a pan, heat the avocado oil over medium heat and sauté the onion and bell pepper for about 8–9 minutes.
2. Add the garlic, thyme, cayenne powder, and salt and sauté for about 1 minute.
3. Add in all remaining Ingredients: and cook until boiling.

4. Now, adjust the heat to low and simmer for about 1 hour or until desired thickness.
5. Serve hot.

Nutrition: Calories 147 Fats 0.3 g Cholesterol 0 mg Carbohydrates 28.2 g Fiber 6.2 g Protein 6.2 g

85.   Chickpeas with Greens

Preparation Time: 15 minutes
Cooking Time: 18 minutes
Servings: 6
Ingredients:

- 2 tablespoons grapeseed oil
- 1 medium onion, chopped
- 4 garlic cloves, minced
- 1 teaspoon dried thyme, crushed
- 1 teaspoon dried oregano, crushed
- ½ teaspoon cayenne powder
- 1 cup tomato, chopped finely
- 2½ cups cooked chickpeas
- 4 cups fresh dandelion greens, chopped
- 2 tablespoons spring water
- 2 tablespoons fresh key lime juice
- Sea salt, as needed
- 3 tablespoons fresh basil, chopped

Directions:

1. In a skillet, heat the grapeseed oil over medium heat and sauté the onion for about 8–9 minutes.
2. Add the garlic, herbs, and cayenne powder and sauté for about 1 minute.
3. Add the greens and water and cook for about 2–3 minutes.
4. Add the tomatoes and chickpeas and cook for about 3–5 minutes.
5. Add in lime juice and salt and stir to combine.
6. Remove the pan of mixture from the heat and serve hot with the garnishing of basil.

Nutrition: Calories 193 Fats 0.6 g Cholesterol 0 mg Carbohydrates 29.9 g Fiber 6.7 g Protein 6.6 g

86.   Quinoa with Mushroom

Preparation Time: 15 minutes
Cooking Time: 30 minutes
Servings: 4
Ingredients:

- ½ tablespoon avocado oil
- 1 cup uncooked quinoa, rinsed
- 12 ounces fresh white mushrooms, sliced

- 3 garlic cloves, minced
- 1¾ cup spring water
- ¼ cup fresh cilantro, chopped
- ¼ teaspoon cayenne powder
- Sea salt, as needed

Directions:
1. Ina medium pan, heat avocado oil over medium-high heat and sauté the garlic for about 30–40 seconds.
2. Add the mushrooms and cook on for about 5–6 minutes, stirring frequently.
3. Stir in the quinoa and cook for about 2 minutes, stirring continuously.
4. Add the water, cayenne, and salt and bring to a boil.
5. Now, adjust the heat to low and simmer, covered for about 15–18 minutes or until almost all the liquid is absorbed.
6. Serve hot with the garnishing of cilantro.

Nutrition: Calories 181 Fats 0.4 g Cholesterol 0 mg Carbohydrates 31 g Fiber 4 g Protein 8.9 g

87. Wild Rice & Squash Pilaf

Preparation Time: 15 minutes
Cooking Time: 45 minutes
Servings: 8

Ingredients:
- 1 medium butternut squash, peeled and cubed
- 1/3 cup avocado oil
- Sea salt, as needed
- 2 cups wild rice, rinsed
- 6 cups spring water
- 1 medium onion, chopped
- 2 garlic cloves, minced
- ¼ cup fresh key lime juice
- ¼ cup fresh orange juice
- 1 teaspoon fresh key lime zest, grated
- ½ teaspoon ground cumin
- ¼ teaspoon ground cinnamon
- ½ teaspoon cayenne pepper
- 1 cup fresh cranberries
- ¾ cup walnuts, chopped
- 3 tablespoons fresh parsley, chopped

Directions:
1. Preheat your oven to 400°F.
2. In a bowl, add the squash cubes, 1 tablespoon of oil, and salt and toss to coat well.
3. Divide the squash cubes onto 2 baking sheets and spread in a single layer.

4. Roast for about 20 minutes.
5. Meanwhile, in a medium skillet, heat 1 tablespoon of oil over medium heat and sauté the onion and garlic for about 3–4 minutes.
6. In a bowl, add the remaining oil, lime juice, orange juice, lime zest, and spices and beat until well combined.
7. In a medium pan, add the water and rice over medium-high heat and bring to a boil.
8. Now, adjust the heat to low and simmer, covered for about 40 minutes.
9. Remove the pan of rice from heat and drain completely.
10. Transfer the cooked rice into a bowl.
11. Add the cooked onion mixture, squash cubes, cranberries, walnuts, parsley, and dressing and gently stir to combine.
12. Serve immediately.

Nutrition: Calories 299 Fats 0.7 g Cholesterol 0 mg Carbohydrates 48.9 g Fiber 7 g Protein 10.3 g

88. Kamut & Quinoa Casserole

Preparation Time: 15 minutes
Cooking Time: 55 minutes
Servings: 6

Ingredients:
- 2½ cups quinoa flour
- 2 cups spring water
- 1 cup cooked Kamut cereal
- ¾ cup onion, chopped
- ½ cup green bell pepper, seeded and chopped
- 2 tablespoons chickpea flour
- 2 tablespoons fresh sage, chopped
- 1 teaspoon dried oregano
- 1 teaspoon dried basil
- 1 teaspoon dried thyme
- 1 tablespoon onion powder
- Sea salt, as needed
- ¼ teaspoon cayenne powder

Directions:
1. Preheat your oven to 350°F.
2. Lightly, grease a glass baking dish.
3. In a bowl, add the flour and water and beat until well combined.
4. Add the remaining Ingredients: and mix until well combined.
5. Place the mixture into the prepared baking dish evenly.
6. Bake for approximately 45–55 minutes.

7. Remove from the oven and set aside to cool slightly before serving.

Nutrition: Calories 223 Fats 0.1 g Cholesterol 0 mg Carbohydrates 38.1 g Fiber 5.4 g Protein 8.5 g

89. Pasta with Mushroom Sauce

Preparation Time: 15 minutes
Cooking Time: 10 minutes
Cooking Time: 25 minutes
Servings: 4
Ingredients:
- 12 ounces spelt pasta
- 4 tablespoons avocado oil
- 1 pound fresh white mushrooms, sliced
- 2 garlic clove, minced
- 2 cups homemade walnut milk
- 2 tablespoons fresh parsley, chopped
- 1½ tablespoons fresh key lime juice
- Sea salt, as needed
- Pinch of cayenne powder

Directions:
1. In a medium saucepan, add salted water and bring to a rolling boil.
2. Add pasta and cook for about 8–10 minutes or according to manufacturer's directions.
3. Meanwhile, in a large skillet, heat 2 tablespoons of the oil over medium heat and sauté the mushroom and garlic for about 4–5 minutes.
4. With a slotted spoon, transfer the mushrooms onto a plate.
5. In the same skillet, heat the remaining oil over medium heat.
6. Slowly, add the flour, beating continuously.
7. Cook for about 1 minute, stirring continuously.
8. Slowly, add the milk, beating continuously until smooth.
9. Add the mushrooms, parsley, lime juice, salt, and cayenne powder and cook for about 1–2 minutes.
10. Divide the pasta onto serving plates.
11. Top with mushroom sauce and serve.

Nutrition: Calories 381 Fats 0.5 g Cholesterol 0 mg Carbohydrates 67 g Fiber 9.9 g Protein 16.6 g

90. Spinach with Chickpeas

Preparation Time: 10 minutes
Cooking Time: 15 minutes
Servings: 2
Ingredients:

- 3 tablespoons extra virgin olive oil
- Sea salt to taste (i.e., Celtic Grey, Himalayan, or Redmond Real Salt)
- 1/2 container grape tomatoes
- 1 large can of chickpeas (rinse well)
- 1 large onion- thinly sliced
- 1 tablespoon grated ginger
- 1 large lemon- zested and freshly juiced
- 1 teaspoon crushed red pepper flakes
- 4 cloves garlic- minced

Directions:
1. Pour the olive oil into a huge skillet and add in the onion. Cook for about 5 minutes until the onion starts to brown.
2. Add in the ginger, lemon zest, garlic, tomatoes, and red pepper flakes, and cook for 3 to 4 minutes.
3. Toss in the chickpeas (rinsed and drained) and cook for an additional 3 to 4 minutes. Now add the spinach in 2 batches, and once it starts to wilt, season with some sea salt and lemon juice.
4. Cook for 2 minutes.
5. Serve!

Nutrition: Calories 178, Fat 8g, Fiber 2g, Carbohydrates 8g, Protein 6g

91. Kale Wraps with Chili and Green Beans

Preparation Time: 30 minutes
Cooking Time: 0 minutes
Servings: 2
Ingredients:
- 1 tablespoon fresh lime juice
- 1 tablespoon raw seed mix
- 2 large kale leaves
- 2 teaspoons fresh garlic (finely chopped)
- Half ripe avocado (pitted and sliced)
- 1 teaspoon fresh red chili (seeded & finely chopped)
- 1 cup fresh cucumber sticks
- Fresh coriander leaves (finely chopped)
- 1 cup green beans

Directions:
1. Spread kale leaves on a clean kitchen work surface.
2. Spread each chopped coriander leaves on each leaf, position them around the end of the leaf, perpendicular to the edge.
3. Spread green beans equally on each leaf, at the edge of each leaf, same as the coriander leaves.

4. Do the same thing with the cucumber sticks.
5. Cut the divide chopped garlic across each leaf, sprinkling it all over the green beans.
6. Cut and share the chopped chili across each leaf and sprinkle it over the garlic.
7. Now, divide the avocado across each leaf, and spread it over chili, garlic, coriander, and green beans.
8. Share the raw seed mix among each leaf, and sprinkle them over other Ingredients:.
9. Divide the lime juice across each leaf and drizzle it over all other Ingredients:.
10. Now fold or roll up the kale leaves and wrap up all the Ingredients: within them.
11. You can serve with soy sauce!

Nutrition: Calories 280, Fat 8g, Fiber 3g, Carbohydrates 8g, Protein 6g

92. Nori Wraps with Fresh Vegetables and Quinoa

Preparation Time: 15 minutes
Cooking Time: 20 minutes
Servings: 1-2
Ingredients:
- 2 nori sheets
- ¼ cup raw carrot sticks
- ½ cup cooked quinoa
- ¼ cup raw carrot sticks
- 1 teaspoon fresh garlic (finely chopped)
- 1 tablespoon raw seed mix
- 1 teaspoon fresh ginger root (finely grated)
- ¼ cup raw cucumber sticks
- ¼ cup fresh coriander leaves (finely chopped)
- 1 tablespoon sesame oilseed

Directions:
1. Get a bowl and mix cooked quinoa with coriander leaves, ginger, seed mix, coriander leaves, and garlic.
2. Pour the sesame oilseed and mix properly.
3. Spread out both nori sheets on two surfaces. Spread the quinoa mix on each of the nori sheets.
4. Add carrot sticks and cucumber on top of the quinoa.
5. Fold up the nori sheets with the quinoa Ingredients: inside.
6. Depending on how you want it, serve with pickled ginger or soy sauce.

Nutrition: Calories 170, Fat 5g, Protein 8g, Carbohydrates 7g

93. Millet Tabbouleh, Lime and Cilantro

Preparation Time: 15 minutes
Cooking Time: 20 minutes
Servings: 6
Ingredients:
- ½ cup lime juice
- ½ cup Cilantro (chopped)
- 5-6 drops Hot sauce (Tabasco)
- ¼ cup Olive oil (and 2 teaspoons divided)
- 2 tomatoes (diced)
- 2 bunches green onions
- 2 cucumber (peeled, seeded and juiced)
- 1 cup millet (rinsed and drained)

Directions:
1. Put oil in a saucepan and heat up over medium heat.
2. Add the millet and fry until it begins to smell fragrant (this takes between three (3) to four (4) minutes).
3. Add about six (6) cups of water and bring to boil.
4. Wait for about fifteen (15) minutes.
5. Turn off the heat, wash and rinse under cold water.
6. Drain the millet and transfer it to a large bowl.
7. Add cucumbers, tomatoes, lime juice, cilantro, green onions, the ¼ cup oil, and hot sauce.
8. Season with pepper and salt to taste.

Nutrition: Calories 200, Fat 8g, Fiber 2g, Carbohydrates 8g, Protein 6g

MAIN DISHES

94. Chickpea Burgers

Preparation Time: 10 minutes
Cooking Time: 20 minutes
Ingredients:

- 2 tablespoons chopped onion
- ¾ cup chickpeas
- ¼ cup cooked quinoa
- 1 tablespoon spring water
- 1 tablespoon grapeseed oil
- Extra:
- 1/3 teaspoon salt
- 1/4 teaspoon cayenne pepper

Directions:

1. Switch on the oven, then set it to 375 degrees F and let it preheat.
2. Meanwhile, place onion, chickpeas, quinoa into a food processor and then pulse little chunky mixture comes together.
3. Add water, salt, and cayenne pepper and then pulse until the dough comes together.
4. Then tip the mixture into a medium bowl, cover it with its lid and then let it rest in the refrigerator for 15 minutes.
5. Shape the mixture into two patties, place them on a baking sheet lined with parchment paper and then bake for 20 minutes, turning halfway.
6. Then switch on the broiler and continue cooking for 2 minutes per side until golden brown.
7. You can serve the patties with spelt flour burgers and tahini butter.

Nutrition: 315.4 Calories; 9.4 g Fats; 10.1 g Protein; 47.7 g

Carbohydrates; 5.8 g Fiber;

95. Chickpea Mashed Potatoes

Preparation Time: 5 minutes
Cooking Time: 30 minutes
Servings: 4
Ingredients:

- 2 cups chickpeas, cooked
- ¼ cup green onions, diced
- 2 teaspoons sea salt
- 2 teaspoons onion powder
- 1 cup walnut milk; homemade, unsweetened

Directions:

1. Plug in a food processor, add chickpeas to it, pour in the milk, and then add salt and onion powder.
2. Cover the blending jar with its lid and then pulse for 1 to 2 minutes until smooth; blend in water if the mixture is too thick.
3. Take a medium saucepan, place it over medium heat, and then add blended chickpea mixture in it.
4. Stir green onions into the chickpeas mixture and then cook the mixture for 30 minutes, stirring constantly.

Nutrition: Calories: 145.8 Carbohydrates: 19.1g Fat: 7.3g Protein: 3.3g

96. Mushroom and Onion Gravy

Preparation Time: 5 minutes
Cooking Time: 18 minutes
Servings: 4
Ingredients:

- 1 cup sliced onions, chopped
- 1 cup mushrooms, sliced
- 2 teaspoons onion powder
- 2 teaspoons sea salt
- 1 teaspoon dried thyme
- 6 tablespoons chickpea flour
- ½ teaspoon cayenne pepper
- 1 teaspoon dried oregano
- 4 tablespoons grapeseed oil
- 4 cups spring water

Directions:

1. Take a medium pot, place it over medium-high heat, add oil and when hot, add onions, mushrooms, and then cook for 1 minute.
2. Season the vegetables with onion powder, salt, thyme, and oregano. Stir until mixed, and cook for 5 minutes.

3. Pour in water, stir in cayenne pepper, stir well, and then bring the mixture to a boil.
4. Slowly stir in chickpea flour, and bring the mixture to a boil again.
5. Remove pan from heat and then serve gravy with a favorite dish.

Nutrition: Calories: 120 Carbohydrates: 8.4g Fat: 7.6g Protein: 2.2g

97. Vegetable Chili

Preparation Time: 5 minutes
Cooking Time: 30 minutes
Servings: 6

Ingredients:
- 2 cups black beans, cooked
- 1 medium red bell pepper; deseeded, chopped
- 1 poblano chili; deseeded, chopped
- 2 jalapeño chilies; deseeded, chopped
- 4 tablespoons cilantro, chopped
- 1 large white onion; peeled, chopped
- 1 ½ tablespoon minced garlic
- 1 ½ teaspoon sea salt
- 1 ½ teaspoon cumin powder
- 1 ½ teaspoon red chili powder
- 3 teaspoons lime juice
- 2 tablespoons grapeseed oil
- 2 ½ cups vegetable stock

Directions:
1. Take a large pot, place it over medium-high heat, add oil and when hot, add onion and cook for 4–5 minutes until translucent.
2. Add bell pepper, jalapeno pepper, poblano chili, and garlic and then cook for 3–4 minutes until veggies turn tender.
3. Season the vegetables with salt, stir in cumin powder and red chili powder, then add chickpeas and pour in vegetable stock.
4. Bring the mixture to a boil, then switch heat to medium-low and simmer the chili for 15–20 minutes until thickened slightly.
5. Then remove the pot from heat, ladle chili stew among six bowls, drizzle with lime juice, garnish with cilantro, and serve.

Nutrition: Calories: 224.2 Carbohydrates: 42.6g Fat: 1.2g Protein: 12.5g

98. Wild Rice and Black Lentils Bowl

Preparation Time: 10 minutes
Cooking Time: 50 minutes
Servings: 4

Ingredients:
- Wild rice
- 2 cups wild rice, uncooked
- 4 cups spring water
- ½ teaspoon salt
- 2 bay leaves
- Black lentils
- 2 cups black lentils, cooked
- 1 ¾ cups coconut milk, unsweetened
- 2 cups vegetable stock
- 1 teaspoon dried thyme
- 1 teaspoon dried paprika
- ½ of medium purple onion; peeled, sliced
- 1 tablespoon minced garlic
- 2 teaspoons creole seasoning
- 1 tablespoon coconut oil
- Plantains
- 3 large plantains, chopped into ¼-inch-thick pieces
- 3 tablespoons coconut oil
- Brussels sprouts
- 10 large brussels sprouts, quartered
- 2 tablespoons spring water
- 1 teaspoon sea salt
- ½ teaspoon ground black pepper

Directions:
1. Prepare the rice: take a medium pot, place it over medium-high heat, pour in water, and add bay leaves and salt.
2. Bring the water to a boil, then switch heat to medium, add rice, and then cook for 30–45 minutes or more until tender.
3. When done, discard the bay leaves from rice, drain if any water remains in the pot, remove it from heat, and fluff by using a fork. Set aside until needed.
4. While the rice boils, prepare lentils: take a large pot, place it over medium-high heat and when hot, add onion and cook for 5 minutes or until translucent.
5. Stir garlic into the onion, cook for 2 minutes until fragrant and golden, then add remaining ingredients for the lentils and stir until mixed.

6. Bring the lentils to a boil, then switch heat to medium and simmer the lentils for 20 minutes until tender, covering the pot with a lid.
7. When done, remove the pot from heat and set aside until needed.
8. While rice and lentils simmer, prepare the plantains: chop them into ¼-inch-thick pieces.
9. Take a large skillet pan, place it over medium heat, add coconut oil and when it melts, add half of the plantain pieces and cook for 7–10 minutes per side or more until golden-brown.
10. When done, transfer browned plantains to a plate lined with paper towels and repeat with the remaining plantain pieces; set aside until needed.
11. Prepare the sprouts: return the skillet pan over medium heat, add more oil if needed, and then add brussels sprouts.
12. Toss the sprouts until coated with oil, and then let them cook for 3–4 minutes per side until brown.
13. Drizzle water over sprouts, cover the pan with the lid, and then cook for 3–5 minutes until steamed.
14. Season the sprouts with salt and black pepper, toss until mixed, and transfer sprouts to a plate.
15. Assemble the bowl: divide rice evenly among four bowls and then top with lentils, plantain pieces, and sprouts.
16. Serve immediately.

Nutrition: Calories: 224.2 Carbohydrates: 42.6g Fat: 1.2g Protein: 12.5g

99. Spaghetti Squash With Peanut Sauce

Preparation Time: 15 minutes
Cooking Time: 15 minutes
Servings: 4
Ingredients:
- 1 cup cooked shelled edamame; frozen, thawed
- 3-pound spaghetti squash
- ½ cup red bell pepper, sliced
- ¼ cup scallions, sliced
- 1 medium carrot, shredded
- 1 teaspoon minced garlic
- ½ teaspoon crushed red pepper
- 1 tablespoon rice vinegar
- ¼ cup coconut aminos
- 1 tablespoon maple syrup
- ½ cup peanut butter
- ¼ cup unsalted roasted peanuts, chopped
- ¼ cup and 2 tablespoons spring water, divided

- ¼ cup fresh cilantro, chopped
- 4 lime wedges

Directions:
1. Prepare the squash: cut each squash in half lengthwise and then remove seeds.
2. Take a microwave-proof dish, place squash halves in it cut-side-up, drizzle with 2 tablespoons water, and then microwave at high heat setting for 10–15 minutes until tender.
3. Let squash cool for 15 minutes until able to handle. Use a fork to scrape its flesh lengthwise to make noodles, and then let noodles cool for 10 minutes.
4. While squash microwaves, prepare the sauce: take a medium bowl, add butter in it along with red pepper and garlic, pour in vinegar, coconut aminos, maple syrup, and water, and then whisk until smooth.
5. When the squash noodles have cooled, distribute them evenly among four bowls, top with scallions, carrots, bell pepper, and edamame beans, and then drizzle with prepared sauce.
6. Sprinkle cilantro and peanuts and serve each bowl with a lime wedge.

Nutrition: Calories: 419 Carbohydrates: 32.8g Fat: 24g Protein: 17.6g

100. Cauliflower Alfredo Pasta

Preparation Time: 10 minutes
Cooking Time: 30 minutes
Servings: 4
Ingredients:
- Alfredo sauce
- 4 cups cauliflower florets, fresh
- 1 tablespoon minced garlic
- ¼ cup nutritional yeast
- ½ teaspoon garlic powder
- ¾ teaspoon sea salt
- ½ teaspoon onion powder
- ½ teaspoon ground black pepper
- ½ tablespoon olive oil
- 1 tablespoon lemon juice, and more as needed for serving
- ½ cup almond milk, unsweetened
- Pasta
- 1 tablespoon minced parsley
- 1 lemon, juiced
- ½ teaspoon sea salt
- ¼ teaspoon ground black pepper
- 12 ounces spelt pasta; cooked, warmed

Directions:

1. Take a large pot half full with water, place it over medium-high heat, and then bring it to a boil.
2. Add cauliflower florets, cook for 10–15 minutes until tender, drain them well, and then return florets to the pot.
3. Take a medium skillet pan, place it over low heat, add oil and when hot, add garlic and cook for 4–5 minutes until fragrant and golden-brown.
4. Spoon garlic into a food processor, add remaining ingredients for the sauce in it, along with cauliflower florets, and then pulse for 2–3 minutes until smooth.
5. Tip the sauce into the pot, stir it well, place it over medium-low heat, and then cook for 5 minutes until hot.
6. Add pasta into the pot, toss well until coated, taste to adjust seasoning, and then cook for 2 minutes until pasta gets hot.
7. Divide pasta and sauce among four plates, season with salt and black pepper, drizzle with lemon juice, and then top with minced parsley.

Nutrition: Calories: 360 Carbohydrates: 59g Fat: 9g Protein: 13g

101. Kale Chickpea Mash

Preparation Time: 15 minutes
Cooking Time: 12 minutes
Servings: 1
Ingredients:

- 1 shallot
- 3 tablespoons garlic
- A bunch of kale
- 1/2 cup boiled chickpea
- 2 tablespoons coconut oil
- Sea salt

Directions:

1. Add some garlic in olive oil
2. Chop shallot and fry it with oil in a nonstick skillet.
3. Cook until the shallot turns golden brown.
4. Add kale and garlic in the skillet and stir well.
5. Add chickpeas and cook for 6 minutes. Add the rest of the ingredients and give a good stir.
6. Serve and enjoy

Nutrition: Calories: 149 Fat: 8g Carbohydrates: 13g Protein: 4g Fiber 3g

102. Quinoa and Apple

Preparation Time: 15 minutes

Cooking Time: 12 minutes
Servings: 1
Ingredients:

- 1/2 cup quinoa
- 1 apple
- 1/2 lemon
- Cinnamon to taste

Directions:

1. Cook quinoa according to the packet directions.
2. Grate the apple and add to the cooked quinoa. Cook for 30 seconds.
3. Serve in a bowl then sprinkle lime and cinnamon. Enjoy.

Nutrition: Calories: 229 Fat: 3.2g Carbohydrates: 32.3g Protein: 6.1g Fiber: 3.3g

103. Kale Caesar Salad

Preparation Time: 5 minutes
Cooking Time: 12 minutes
Servings: 1
Ingredients:

- 1 bunch of curly kale, washed
- 1 cup sunflower seeds
- 1/3 cup almond nuts
- 1/8 tablespoon chipotle powder
- 2 garlic cloves
- 1-1/4 water
- 1-1/2 tablespoon agave syrup
- 1/2 tablespoon sea salt

Directions:

1. Wash and pat dry the curly kale and remove the center membrane .tear the kale leaves into small sizes.
2. Add all other ingredients in a blender and blend until smooth and creamy.
3. Pour half of the mixture over the kale and toss until well coated.
4. Pour the remaining mixture and mix until the kales are well coated on the curls and folds.
5. Let rest for 10 minutes then serve on plates. Sprinkle sunflower seeds and enjoy.

Nutrition: Calories: 157 Fat: 6g Carbohydrates: 18g Protein: 9g Fiber: 2g

104. Red and White Salad

Preparation Time: 5 minutes
Cooking Time: 10 minutes
Servings: 2

Ingredients:
- 3 radishes
- 1 fennel bulb, greens removed
- 1/2 jicama, peeled and halved
- 2 celery stalks
- Juice from 1 lime
- 1/4 cup avocado oil
- Salt to taste
- Macadamia nuts

Directions:
1. Slice radish, fennel, jicama, and celery using a mandolin slicer on the thinnest setting.
2. Toss them in a mixing bowl with lime and oil. Season with salt then top with nuts.
3. Enjoy.

Nutrition: Calories: 197 Fat: 9g Carbohydrates: 20g Protein: 7g Fiber: 2g

105. Almond Milk

Preparation Time: 5 minutes
Cooking Time: 10 minutes
Servings: 2
Ingredients:
- 1.7oz almonds, sliced
- 133.8 oz filtered water
- 1 tablespoon sunflower granules
- 2 dates, stones removed

Directions:
1. Soak the almonds for a few hours ahead of Time.
2. Add all the ingredients in a blender and blend for 2 minutes.
3. Pour the milk in a container through a straining cloth. Carry in your lunch box or store in a fridge for up to 3 days.
4. You can use almond pulp in cakes or almond mixes.

Nutrition: Calories: 90 Fat: 2.5g Carbohydrates: 16g Protein: 1g

106. Creamy Kale Salad With Avocado and Tomato

Preparation Time: 5 minutes
Cooking Time: 10 minutes
Servings: 2
Ingredients:
- 2 handful of kale
- 2 cherry tomatoes

- 1 ripe avocado
- Juice from 1 lime
- 1 garlic clove, crushed
- 1 tablespoon agave
- 1/2 tablespoon paprika
- 1/2 tablespoon black pepper

Directions:
1. Wash kale and tomatoes and roughly chop them. Place them in a mixing bowl.
2. Peel the avocado and add it to the mixing bowl.
3. Add lemon juice and the rest of the ingredients to the bowl and mix them thoroughly.
4. Serve and enjoy.

Nutrition: Calories: 179.2 Fat: 14.1g Carbohydrates: 13.5g Protein: 3.7g Fiber: 6.1g

107. Caprese Stuffed Avocado

Preparation Time: 5 minutes
Cooking Time: 10 minutes
Servings: 4
Ingredients:
- 1/2 cup cherry tomatoes
- 4 0z baby bocconcini balls
- 2 tablespoons basil pesto
- 1 tablespoon minced garlic
- 1/4 oil
- Salt and pepper to taste
- 2 ripe avocados
- 2 tablespoons balsamic glaze
- Basil for serving

Directions:
1. In a mixing bowl, add cherry tomatoes, bocconcini balls, basil pesto, garlic, salt and pepper to taste. Toss until well combined and all flavors have blended.
2. Half the avocados and arrange them on a platter.
3. Spoon the mixture in the avocado halves and drizzle with balsamic glaze.
4. Top with basil and serve. Enjoy.

Nutrition: Calories: 341 Fat: 29g Carbohydrates: 15g Protein: 8g Fiber: 6g

108. Tef Burger

Preparation Time: 10 minute
Cooking Time: 8 minutes
Ingredients
- ¾ cup cooked tef grains

- ¾ cup chickpea flour
- 2 tablespoons diced onion
- 2 tablespoons diced red bell pepper
- ½ teaspoon dill
- Extra:
- ¼ teaspoon salt
- ½ teaspoon oregano
- 1/8 teaspoon cayenne pepper
- ½ teaspoon basil
- 1 tablespoon grapeseed oil

Directions

1. Take a medium pan, place over medium-heat, then add oil and when hot, add onion and bell pepper and cook for 3 minutes until tender.
2. Transfer vegetables into the large bowl, add remaining ingredients, stir until mixed, and then shape the mixture into patties.
3. Place patties into the pan and then cook for 3 minutes per side until crisp and golden brown on all sides.
4. Storage instructions:
5. Cool the patties, divide evenly between two containers, cover with a lid, and then store the containers in the refrigerator for up to 7 days.
6. Reheating instructions:
7. When ready to eat, reheat in the oven for 1 to 2 minutes until hot and then serve.

Nutrition: 122 Calories; 4.1 g Fats; 4.2 g Protein; 16.6 g Carbohydrates; 2.6 g Fiber;

109. Vegan Rib Roast

Preparation Time: 10 minutes
Cooking Time: 15 minutes
Ingredients:

- 2 caps of Portobello mushrooms, ½ -inch thick sliced
- 1 teaspoon of sea salt
- ½ cup Alkaline Barbecue Sauce
- 1 teaspoon onion powder
- ¼ cup spring water
- Extra:
- ½ teaspoon cayenne pepper
- 1 tablespoon grapeseed oil

Directions:

1. Place mushroom slices in a container with a lid, add BBQ sauce, all the seasoning, and water, cover with a lid, and then shake until coated.

2. Place the container into the refrigerator and then let it marinate for a minimum of 6 hours, shaking every 2 hours.
3. When ready to cook, take a griddle pan, place it over medium-high heat, brush with oil and let it preheat.
4. Thread three slices of mushrooms in a skewer, then arrange these skewers on the pan and then cook for 15 minutes, flipping every 3 minutes.

Nutrition: 108 Calories; 0.6 g Fats; 6 g Protein; 18 g Carbohydrates; 3 g Fiber;

110. Revitalizing Chickpea Dish

Preparation Time: 10 minutes
Cooking Time: 0 minutes
Ingredients:

- ¼ cup diced red onion
- 2 cups cooked chickpeas
- 1/8 cup diced green bell pepper
- ¼ teaspoon of sea salt
- 2 teaspoons onion powder
- Extra:
- ¼ teaspoon salt
- 1/8 teaspoon cayenne pepper
- 2/3 cup alkaline hemp seed mayo
- 1 teaspoon dill
- ½ nori sheet, cut into small pieces

Directions:

1. Take a large bowl, place chickpeas in it, and then mash them by using a fork.
2. Add remaining Ingredients:, stir until well mixed and then chill the salad for a minimum of 30 minutes.

Nutrition: 259 Calories; 13.7 g Fats; 6.1 g Protein; 27.7 g Carbohydrates; 5.2 g Fiber;

111. Tef Grain Burger

Preparation Time: 10 minutes
Cooking Time: 8 minutes
Ingredients:

- ¾ cup cooked tef grains
- ¾ cup chickpea flour
- 2 tablespoons diced onion
- 2 tablespoons diced red bell pepper
- ½ teaspoon dill
- Extra:
- ¼ teaspoon salt

- ½ teaspoon oregano
- 1/8 teaspoon cayenne pepper
- ½ teaspoon basil
- 1 tablespoon grapeseed oil

Directions:
1. Take a medium skillet pan, place it over medium heat, add oil and when hot, add onion and bell pepper and cook for 3 minutes until tender.
2. Transfer vegetables into the large bowl, add remaining Ingredients:, stir until mixed, and then shape the mixture into patties.
3. Place patties into the pan and then cook for 3 minutes per side until crisp and golden brown on all sides.

Nutrition: 122 Calories; 4.1 g Fats; 4.2 g Protein; 16.6 g Carbohydrates; 2.6 g Fiber;

112. Zoodles with Basil & Avocado Sauce

Preparation Time: 10 minutes
Cooking Time: 0 minutes
Ingredients:
- 2 zucchinis, spiralized into noodles
- 2 avocados, peeled, pitted
- ½ cup walnuts
- 2 cups basil leaves
- 24 cherry tomatoes, sliced
- Extra:
- 1/3 teaspoon salt
- 4 tablespoons key lime juice
- ½ cup spring water

Directions:
1. Prepare the sauce and for this, place all the Ingredients: except for zucchini noodles and tomatoes in a food processor and then pulse until smooth.
2. Take a large bowl, place zucchini noodles in it, add tomato slices, pour in the prepared sauce and then toss until coated.

Nutrition: 330 Calories; 20.7 g Fats; 7.1 g Protein; 35.3 g Carbohydrates; 7.8 g Fiber;

113. Butternut Squash and Apple Burger

Preparation Time: 10 minutes
Cooking Time: 1 hour;
Ingredients:

- ¾ cup diced butternut squash
- ½ cup diced apples
- 1 cup cooked wild rice
- ¼ cup chopped shallots
- ½ tablespoon thyme
- Extra:
- ¼ teaspoon sea salt, divided
- 1 tablespoon pumpkin seeds, unsalted
- 1 tablespoon grapeseed oil
- 2 spelt burgers, halved, toasted

Directions:
1. Switch on the oven, then set it to 400 degrees F and let it preheat.
2. Meanwhile, take a cookie sheet, line it with parchment sheet, spread squash pieces on it and then sprinkle with 1/8 teaspoon salt.
3. Bake the squash for 15 minutes, then add shallots and apple, sprinkle with remaining salt, and then bake for 20 to 30 minutes until cooked.
4. When done, let the vegetable mixture cool for 15 minutes, transfer it into a food processor, add thyme and then pulse until a chunky mixture comes together.
5. Add pumpkin seeds and cooked wild rice, pulse until combined, and then tip the mixture in a bowl.
6. Taste the mixture to adjust and then shape it into two patties.
7. Take a skillet pan, place it over medium heat, add oil and when hot, place patties in it and then cook for 5 to 7 minutes per side until browned.
8. Sandwich patties in burger buns and then serve.

Nutrition: 250 Calories; 4 g Fats; 6 g Protein; 51 g Carbohydrates; 5 g Fiber;

114. Kale and "Awevocado" Dish

Preparation Time: 5 minutes
Cooking Time: 0 minutes
Ingredients:
- 1 bundle of kale, cut into thin strips
- 1 small white onion, peeled, chopped
- 12 cherry tomatoes, chopped
- 1 tablespoon salt
- 1 avocado, peeled, pitted, sliced

Directions:
1. Take a large bowl, place kale strips in it, sprinkle with salt, and then massage for 2 minutes.
2. Cover the bowl with a plastic wrap or its lid, let it rest for a minimum of 30 minutes, and then stir in onion and tomatoes until well combined.

3. Let the salad sit for 5 minutes, add avocado slices, and then serve.

Nutrition: 143 Calories; 10.5 g Fats; 3 g Protein; 12.4 g Carbohydrates; 4.8 g Fiber;

115. Zucchini 'Bacon' Dish

Preparation Time: 10 minutes
Cooking Time: 20 minutes
Ingredients:

- 2 zucchini, cut into strips
- 1 tablespoon onion powder
- 1 tablespoon of sea salt
- ½ teaspoon cayenne powder
- Extra:
- ¼ cup date
- 2 tablespoons agave syrup
- 1 teaspoon liquid smoke
- ¼ cup spring water
- 1 tablespoon grapeseed oil

Directions:

1. Take a medium saucepan, place it over medium heat, add all the Ingredients: except for zucchini and oil and then cook until
2. has dissolved.
3. Then place zucchini strips in a large bowl, pour in the mixture from the saucepan, toss until coated, and then let it marinate for a minimum of 1 hour.
4. When ready to cook, switch on the oven, set it to 400 degrees F, and let it preheat.
5. Take a baking sheet, line it with parchment sheet, grease with oil, arrange marinated zucchini strips on it, and then bake for 10 minutes.
6. Then flip the zucchini, continue cooking for 4 minutes and then let cool completely.

Nutrition: 184 Calories; 2 g Fats; 12 g Protein; 26 g Carbohydrates; 2 g Fiber;

116. Savory Walnut Meat

Preparation Time: 5 minutes
Cooking Time: 15 minutes
Ingredients:

- 8 ounces walnuts, soaked overnight
- ¼ cup sliced green bell peppers
- ½ cup sliced white onions
- ¼ cup sliced red bell peppers
- ¼ cup sliced orange bell peppers
- Extra:

- 1 tablespoon onion powder
- ½ teaspoon of sea salt
- 1 teaspoon dried oregano
- ¼ teaspoon cayenne pepper
- 1 teaspoon dried basil
- 2 tablespoons grapeseed oil
- 2 tablespoons spring water

Directions:

1. Drain the walnuts, place them in a food processor, and then pulse until crumbled.
2. Take a skillet pan, place it over medium-high heat, add oil and when hot, add onions and all the peppers, stir in all the seasoning and then cook for 10 minutes until tender.
3. Add walnuts, stir in water and then cook for 3 to 5 minutes until hot.
4. Serve meat with cooked spelt pasta.

Nutrition: 240 Calories; 23.7 g Fats; 5.7 g Protein; 5.6 g Carbohydrates; 2.7 g Fiber;

117. Amaranth Bowl with Butternut Squash

Preparation Time: 5 minutes
Cooking Time: 10 minutes
Ingredients:

- 10 ounces cooked butter squash chunks
- 1 apple, peeled, cored, sliced
- 8 ounces collard greens
- 1 teaspoon garam masala
- 1 ½ cup cooked amaranth
- Extra:
- ½ teaspoon salt
- ¼ teaspoon cayenne pepper
- 1 teaspoon and 1 tablespoon grapeseed oil

Directions:

1. Take a pan, place it over medium heat, add 1 teaspoon oil and when hot, add squash piece, sprinkle with garam masala and ¼ teaspoon salt, stir until mixed and then cook for 5 minutes until hot.
2. Transfer squash mixture to a bowl, return skillet over medium heat, add remaining oil and when hot, add collard green, season with remaining salt, and then cook for 5 minutes until hot.
3. Divide amaranth between two bowls, top with apple, collards, and squash mixture and then serve.

Nutrition: 325 Calories; 12 g Fats; 9.2 g Protein; 50 g Carbohydrates; 8.1 g Fiber;

118. Alkaline Hot Dogs

Preparation Time: 5 minutes
Cooking Time: 10 minutes
Ingredients:

- 1 cup cooked chickpeas
- 1/3 cup diced green bell pepper,
- 1 cup spelt flour
- 1/3 cup diced white onion,
- 1 teaspoon coriander
- Extra:
- ¼ cup diced shallots,
- 1 tablespoon onion powder
- 2 teaspoons sea salt
- ½ teaspoon dill
- 1 tablespoon grapeseed oil
- ½ cup liquid from chickpeas

Directions:

1. Take a pan, place it over medium heat, add oil and when hot, add chickpeas and all the vegetables and then cook for 5 minutes.
2. Transfer the chickpeas and vegetables in a food processor, add remaining Ingredients: and pulse until well combined.
3. Shape the mixture into hot dog shape rolls, and then wrap each hot dog in a parchment paper.
4. Boil some water in a pot, place a steamer on it, arrange wrapped hot dogs on it and then steam for 30 minutes.
5. When done, uncover the hot dogs and then fry for 10 minutes over medium heat until browned on all sides.
6. Serve hot dogs in spelt buns.

Nutrition: 120 Calories; 2 g Fats; 16 g Protein; 8 g Carbohydrates; 2 g Fiber;

119. Teff Sausage

Preparation Time: 10 minutes
Cooking Time: 6 minutes
Ingredients:

- 2 tablespoons diced onions
- ¾ cup cooked teff grain
- 2 tablespoons diced red bell pepper
- ¼ cup chickpea flour
- 1 teaspoon basil
- Extra:
- 1 teaspoon oregano
- ½ teaspoon of sea salt

- ¼ teaspoon crushed red pepper
- 1 tablespoon grapeseed oil

Directions:

1. Take a medium skillet pan, place it over medium-high heat, add oil and when hot, add onion and peppers, and then cook for 2 to 3 minutes until tender.
2. Stir in chickpea flour, transfer the mixture into a medium bowl, add remaining Ingredients:, stir until well mixed, and then shape the mixture into evenly sized patties.
3. Return skillet pan over medium heat and when hot, place patties on it and then cook for 3 minutes per side until crisp and cooked.

Nutrition: 88.3 Calories; 2.3 g Fats; 4.6 g Protein; 12.7 g Carbohydrates; 1.6 g Fiber;

120. Creamy Avocado Cilantro Lime Dressing Recipe

Preparation Time: 20 minutes
Cooking Time: 10 minutes
Servings: 6-8
Ingredients:

- ¼ cup olive oil
- ¼ teaspoon of sea salt
- ½ cup cilantro, chopped
- ¼ cup plain goat yogurt
- Juice of ½ lime
- 1 teaspoon lime zest
- 1 avocado
- 1 clove garlic, peeled
- ½ jalapeno, chopped
- ¼ teaspoon pepper
- ½ teaspoon cumin

Directions:

1. Place/put all the ingredients in a food processor or mixer and mix it until well balanced.

Nutrition: Calories: 123 Protein: 1g Fat: 12g Carbohydrates: 3.6g

121. Creamy Avocado Dressing

Preparation Time: 5 min
Cooking Time: 5 min
Servings: 4
Ingredients:

- 1/4 teaspoon ground black pepper
- Water, as needed

- 1 whole large avocado
- 1 clove garlic, peeled
- 1/2 tablespoon fresh lime or lemon juice
- 3 tablespoons olive oil or avocado oil
- 1/4 teaspoon kosher salt

Directions:
1. Put the peeled clove of garlic, lime or lemon juice, avocado, olive oil, salt, and pepper into a mini food processor.
2. Process till smooth, stopping a few Times to scrape the sides down. Thin the salad dressing out with some water (1/4 cup to 1/2 cup) before a perfect consistency is achieved.
3. Maintain/keep at least a week in an airtight container, but 3 to 4 days is best.

Nutrition: Calories: 38.2 Fat: 2.6g Cholesterol: 1.2mg Carbohydrates: 3.6g Fiber: 1.0g

122. Southwestern Avocado Salad Dressing

Preparation Time: 5 minutes
Cooking Time: 1 hour
Servings: 8
Ingredients:
- 1 ripe avocado
- 1 cup buttermilk
- 1/2 teaspoon garlic powder
- 1/2 teaspoon chipotle chili powder
- 1/2 teaspoon salt
- 1/4 cup cilantro
- Juice of 1/2 lime
- 1 teaspoon ranch seasoning powder homemade or store-bought

Directions:
1. Break the avocado in half, extract the pit from the flesh and scoop the skin.
2. Attach all the other ingredients together to a mixer.
3. Blend in until creamy and smooth.
4. Prior to serving, refrigerate for one hour.
5. Keeps in the refrigerator for 3 days.

Nutrition: Calories: 61 Fat: 4g Cholesterol: 3mg Carbohydrates: 4g Fiber: 1g Protein: 1g

123. Brain-Boosting Smoothie Recipe

Preparation Time: 5 minutes
Cooking Time: 5 minutes

Servings: 1
Ingredients:
- ½ avocado
- ½ banana
- ½ cup blueberries
- 6 walnuts
- 1 scoop vanilla whey protein powder
- ½ cup of water

Directions:
1. Add/put all ingredients to blender then blend until a smooth texture is reached.

Nutrition: Calories: 400 Fat: 13g Protein: 7g Carbohydrates: 68g Fiber: 10g

124. Lemon Avocado Salad Dressing

Preparation Time: 5 minutes
Cooking Time: 5 minutes
Servings: 2-3
Ingredients:
- 2 tablespoons olive oil
- 1 garlic clove, minced
- 1/2 teaspoon seasoned salt
- 1 medium ripe avocado, peeled and mashed
- 1/4 cup water
- 2 tablespoons sour cream
- 2 tablespoons lemon juice
- 1 tablespoon minced fresh dill or 1 teaspoon dill weed
- 1/2 teaspoon honey
- Salad greens, cherry tomatoes, sliced cucumbers, and sweet red and yellow pepper strips

Directions:
1. In a blender, combine the first nine ingredients; cover and process until blended.
2. Serve with salad greens, tomatoes, cucumbers, and peppers. Store in the refrigerator.

Nutrition: Calories: 38.2 Fat: 2.6 g Cholesterol: 1.2mg Carbohydrates: 3.6g Fiber: 1.0g Protein: 0.8g

125. Avocado Salad With Bell Pepper and Tomatoes

Preparation Time: 5 minutes
Cooking Time: 5 minutes
Servings: 2-3
Ingredients:

- Coarse salt
- 1 firm, ripe avocado, halved and pitted
- 6 cherry tomatoes, halved
- 1 teaspoon extra-virgin olive oil
- Juice of 1/2 lime
- 1 scallions, trimmed and thinly sliced
- 1 tablespoon chopped fresh cilantro leaves, with whole leaves for garnish
- 1 small garlic clove, minced
- Pinch of cayenne pepper
- 1/2 yellow bell pepper, ribs & seeds removed, diced

Directions:
1. Whisk the olive oil, lime juice, garlic, and cayenne together in a small bowl. Season with the salt.
2. From the avocado halves, scoop out the flesh, conserve shells, and chop. Switch to a bowl and add chopped cilantro, bell pepper, onions, scallion
3. Drizzle with salt and season with dressing. Stir gently to mix. Mix spoon into allocated containers. Garnish with whole leaves of cilantro and serve right away.

Nutrition: Calories: 424 Fiber: 16.36g Fat: 5g Carbohydrates: 31.25g Fat: 34.63g Protein: 6.6g

126. **Avocado Salad**

Preparation Time: 10 minutes
Cooking Time: 5 minutes
Servings: 4
Ingredients:
- 1 avocado, finely chopped
- 3 tablespoons boiled corn
- 1 tomato, thinly chopped
- 1 tablespoon extra-virgin olive oil
- Salt to taste
- 1 tablespoon lemon juice
- 3 green onions, chopped

Directions:
1. In a large bowl, whisk in chopped avocado and lemon juice.
2. In the same bowl, mix it with other ingredients, except for tomato.
3. Serve on slices of bread with sliced tomatoes.

Nutrition: Calories: 164.2 Fat: 11.8g Cholesterol: 10.0mg Carbohydrates: 11.6g Fiber: 4.7g Protein: 5.4g

127. **Avocado Seitan Salad With Arugula**

Preparation Time: 10 minutes
Cooking Time: 5 minutes
Servings: 1
Ingredients:
- 2 green onions, sliced thinly
- 8 cherry tomatoes, halved (or a mix of yellow and red)
- ¾ pound seitan fillet
- 1 avocado, pitted, peeled and chopped
- 1 small (raw) zucchini, thinly sliced in half-moons
- 4 radishes, thinly sliced
- 1 recipe avocado citrus dressing

Directions:
1. Preheat to 400 ° f on the oven. Line a small saucepan with parchment paper.
2. Arrange the seitan on the pan, skin down, and bake for 10 to 12 minutes until just cooked.
3. Warm slightly, cut fat, flake flesh, and set aside.
4. Divide arugula between serving plates. Top with seitan and avocado, courgettes, red onion, and tomatoes.
5. Serve in citrus dressing with creamy avocado

Nutrition: Calories: 320 Fat: 32g Cholesterol: 5mg Carbohydrates: 6g Fiber: 3g Protein: 6g

128. **Herbal Smoothie**

Preparation Time: 5 minutes
Cooking Time: 0 minutes
Ingredients
- 2 cups herbal tea
- 1 burro banana, peeled
- 1 tablespoon walnut
- 1 tablespoon agave syrup

Directions
1. Plug in a high-speed food processor or blender and add all the ingredients in its jar.
2. Cover the blender jar with its lid and then pulse for 40 to 60 seconds until smooth.
3. Divide the drink between two glasses and then serve.
4. Storage instructions:
5. Divide drink between two jars or bottles, cover with a lid and then store the containers in the refrigerator for up to 3 days.

Nutrition: 75.5 Calories; 2.1 g Fats; 0.9 g Protein; 13.2 g Carbohydrates; 1.8 g Fiber;

129. Amaranth with Walnuts

Preparation Time: 10 minutes
Cooking Time: 30 minutes
Ingredients:

- 1 cup amaranth
- 2 cups of spring water
- ¼ teaspoon salt
- 2 tablespoons chopped walnuts
- 2 tablespoons agave syrup

Directions:

1. Take a mediums saucepan, place it over medium-high heat, add amaranth, pour in water, and then bring it to a boil.
2. Then switch heat to medium level, cook it for 25 minutes until all the liquid has been absorbed, and then stir in salt.
3. Remove pan from heat, let amaranth rest for 10 minutes, and divide evenly between two bowls and then top with nuts and agave syrup.

Nutrition: 175 Calories; 0 g Fats; 1.3 g Protein; 42 g Carbohydrates; 4 g Fiber;

130. Spiced Amaranth Patties

Preparation Time: 10 minutes
Cooking Time: 12 minutes
Ingredients:

- ½ cup amaranth, cooked
- ½ of medium white onion, peeled, chopped
- ¼ cup grated zucchini
- ¼ cup chopped red bell pepper
- Extra:
- 1/3 teaspoon salt
- ¼ teaspoon cayenne pepper
- ¼ teaspoon coriander powder
- ¼ teaspoon key lime zest
- 2 tablespoons grapeseed oil

Directions:

1. Take a small frying pan, place it over medium heat, add 1 tablespoon oil and when hot, add onion and then cook for 5 minutes until tender.
2. Add zucchini and red pepper, stir until mixed and cook for 3 minutes.
3. Add remaining Ingredients: except for oil and amaranth, stir until mixed, then remove the pan from heat and cool for 10 minutes.
4. Take a medium bowl, place cooked amaranth in it, add vegetable mixture, stir until combined, and then shape the mixture into evenly sized patties.

5. Take a large skillet pan, place it over medium heat, add remaining oil and when hot, place patties in it and then cook for 3 minutes per side until golden brown.

Nutrition: 148 Calories; 2 g Fats; 10 g Protein; 24 g Carbohydrates; 8 g Fiber;

131. Amaranth Vegetable Patties

Preparation Time: 10 minutes
Cooking Time: 40 minutes
Ingredients:

- ½ of medium white onion, peeled, minced
- ½ cup amaranth, cooked
- 1 medium zucchini, grated
- ¼ cup chopped basil
- 1 ½ cups Kale, chopped
- Extra:
- ¼ cup chopped dill
- 2 tablespoons spelt flour
- ½ teaspoon salt
- ¼ teaspoon cayenne pepper
- 1 tablespoon olive oil
- 1 ½ tablespoon tahini
- 1 tablespoon key lime juice

Directions:

1. Switch on the oven, then set it to 400 degrees F and let it preheat.
2. Meanwhile, take a skillet pan, place it over medium heat, add oil and when hot, add onion and cook for 5 minutes until tender.
3. Add zucchini, cook for 3 to 5 minutes until soft, then add Kale and cook for 5 minutes until wilted.
4. Spoon the mixture into a bowl, add remaining Ingredients:, stir until mixed, and then shape the mixture into evenly sized patties.
5. Arrange patties onto a baking sheet and then bake for 15 minutes per side until golden brown and cooked.

Nutrition: 152 Calories; 3 g Fats; 7 g Protein; 29 g Carbohydrates; 6 g Fiber;

132. Brussel Sprouts and Quinoa Salad

Preparation Time: 5 minutes
Cooking Time: 0 minutes
Ingredients:

- ¼ cup quinoa, cooked

- ½ pound Brussel sprouts, halved, diced, roasted
- 2 tablespoons dried cranberries
- 1 medium white onion, peeled, sliced caramelized
- Extra:
- 1/3 teaspoon salt
- 1/8 teaspoon cayenne pepper
- ½ of orange, juiced
- ½ teaspoon orange zest
- 1 tablespoon key lime juice

Directions:
1. Take a small bowl, pour orange juice and lime juice in it, add orange zest and then stir until mixed.
2. Take a salad bowl, place remaining Ingredients: in it, drizzle with the orange juice mixture and then toss until mixed.

Nutrition: 190 Calories; 12 g Fats; 5 g Protein; 18 g Carbohydrates; 3 g Fiber;

133. Burritos

Preparation Time: 10 minutes
Cooking Time: 0 minutes
Ingredients:
- 1 avocado, peeled, sliced
- 1 cucumber, deseeded, cut into round slices
- 1 zucchini, sliced
- 2 teaspoons sprouted hemp seeds
- 2 nori sheets
- Extra:
- 1 tablespoon tahini butter
- 2 teaspoons sesame seeds

Directions:
1. Working on one nori sheet at a Time, place it on a cutting board shiny-side-down and then arrange half of each avocado, cucumber and zucchini slices and tahini on it, leaving 1-inch wide spice to the right.
2. Then start folding the sheet over the fillings from the edge that is closest to you, cut into thick slices, and then sprinkle with 1 teaspoon of sesame seeds.
3. Repeat with the remaining nori sheet, and then serve.

Nutrition: 90 Calories; 1.5 g Fats; 1.5 g Protein; 12.5 g Carbohydrates; 1 g Fiber;

134. Vegan Portobello Burgers

Preparation Time: 10 minutes
Cooking Time: 20 minutes

Serving: 4
Ingredients:
- 2 Portobello mushroom caps
- ½ of avocado, sliced
- 1 cup purslane
- 2 teaspoons dried basil
- 2 tablespoons olive oil
- Extra:
- ¼ teaspoon salt
- 1 teaspoon dried oregano
- ½ teaspoon cayenne pepper

Directions:
1. Switch on the oven, then set it to 425 degrees F and let it preheat.
2. Prepare the marinade and for this, take a small bowl, pour in oil, add cayenne pepper, onion powder, oregano, and basil and then stir until mixed.
3. Take a cookie sheet, line it with a foil, brush with oil, place mushroom caps on it, evenly pour the marinade over mushroom caps and then let them marinate for 10 minutes.
4. Then bake the mushroom caps for 20 minutes, flipping halfway, until tender and cooked.
5. When done, place mushroom caps on two plates, top the caps with avocado and purslane evenly and then serve.

Nutrition: 354 Calories; 32.8 g Fats; 3.7 g Protein; 14.4 g Carbohydrates; 4.4 g Fiber;

135. Wakame Salad

Preparation Time: 15 minutes
Cooking Time: 0 minutes
Ingredients
- 1 cup wakame stems
- ½ tablespoon chopped red bell pepper
- ½ teaspoon onion powder
- ½ tablespoon key lime juice
- Extra:
- ½ tablespoon agave syrup
- ½ tablespoon sesame seeds
- ½ tablespoon sesame oil

Directions
1. Place wakame stems in a bowl, cover with water, let them soak for 10 minutes, and then drain.
2. Meanwhile, prepare the dressing and for this, take a small bowl, add lime juice, onion powder, agave syrup and sesame oil in it and then whisk until blended.

3. Place drained wakame stems in a large dish, add bell pepper, pour in the dressing and then toss until coated.
4. Sprinkle sesame seeds over the salad and then serve.
5. Storage instructions:
6. Divide the salad evenly between two meal prep containers, cover with a lid, and then store the containers in the refrigerator for up to 5 days.

Nutrition: 106 Calories; 7.3 g Fats; 3 g Protein; 8 g Carbohydrates; 1.7 g Fiber;

136. Portobello Burgers

Preparation Time: 10 minutes
Cooking Time: 20 minutes
Serving: 2
Ingredients
- 2 Portobello mushroom caps
- ½ of avocado, sliced
- 1 cup purslane
- 2 teaspoons dried basil
- 2 tablespoons olive oil
- Extra:
- ¼ teaspoon salt
- 1 teaspoon dried oregano
- ½ teaspoon cayenne pepper

Directions
1. Switch on the oven, then set it to 425 degrees F and let it preheat.
2. Prepare the marinade and for this, take a small bowl, pour in oil, add cayenne pepper, onion powder, oregano, and basil and then stir until mixed.
3. Take a cookie sheet, line it with a foil, brush with oil, place mushroom caps on it, evenly pour the marinade over mushroom caps and then let them marinate for 10 minutes.
4. Then bake the mushroom caps for 20 minutes, flipping halfway, until tender and cooked.
5. When done, place mushroom caps on two plates, top the caps with avocado and purslane evenly.
6. Storage instructions:
7. Cool the mushroom caps, cover them in a plastic wrap and foil, and then store the containers in the refrigerator for up to 7 days.
8. Reheating instructions:
9. When ready to eat, reheat in the oven for 1 to 2 minutes until hot, top the caps with avocado and purslane evenly and then serve.

Nutrition: 354 Calories; 32.8 g Fats; 3.7 g Protein; 14.4 g

Carbohydrates; 4.4 g Fiber;

137. Green Pancakes

Preparation Time: 10 minutes
Cooking Time: 6 minutes
Ingredients
- ½ cup chickpea flour
- ¼ cup blueberries
- 1 burro banana, peeled
- ½ cup amaranth greens
- ½ cup spring water
- Extra:
- ½ teaspoon of sea salt
- 1 tablespoon agave syrup
- 1 tablespoon walnut butter
- 1 tablespoon grapeseed oil

Directions
1. Plug in a high-speed food processor or blender and add all the ingredients in its jar.
2. Cover the blender jar with its lid, pulse for 40 to 60 seconds until smooth, tip the mixture in a bowl and let it rest for 10 minutes.
3. When ready to cook, take a large frying pan, place it over medium-high heat, add oil and then let it heat.
4. Scoop prepared batter into the hot pan into six portions, shape each portion like a pancake and then cook for 2 to 3 minutes per side until edges have cooked and firm.
5. Storage instructions:
6. Cool the pancakes, divide evenly between two meal prep containers, cover with a lid, and then store the containers in the refrigerator for up to 7 days.
7. Reheating instructions:
8. When ready to eat, reheat in the oven for 1 to 2 minutes until hot and then serve.

Nutrition: 144 Calories; 0.6 g Fats; 6 g Protein; 31.6 g Carbohydrates; 5.4 g Fiber;

138. Grilled Lettuce Salad

Preparation Time: 10 minutes
Cooking Time: 10 minutes
Ingredients
- 2 small heads of romaine lettuce, cut in half
- 1 tablespoon chopped basil
- 1 tablespoon chopped red onion
- ¼ teaspoon onion powder
- ½ tablespoon agave syrup

- Extra:
- ½ teaspoon salt
- ¼ teaspoon cayenne pepper
- 2 tablespoons olive oil
- 1 tablespoon key lime juice

Directions

1. Take a large skillet pan, place it over medium heat and when warmed, arrange lettuce heads in it, cut-side down, and then cook for 4 to 5 minutes per side until golden brown on both sides.
2. When done, transfer lettuce heads to a plate and then let them cool for 5 minutes.
3. Meanwhile, prepare the dressing and for this, place remaining ingredients in a small bowl and then stir until combined.
4. Drizzle the dressing over lettuce heads.
5. Storage instructions:
6. Cool the lettuce, divide evenly between two meal prep containers, cover with a lid, and then store the containers in the refrigerator for up to 7 days. Store the dressing in a mini meal prep container.
7. Reheating instructions:
8. When ready to eat, reheat in the microwave oven for 1 to 2 minutes until ho, drizzle with dressing and then serve.

Nutrition: 130 Calories; 2 g Fats; 2 g Protein; 24 g Carbohydrates; 4 g Fiber;

139. **Vegetable Fajitas Tacos**

Preparation Time: 10 minutes
Cooking Time: 8 minutes
Ingredients

- 2 Portobello mushroom caps, 1/3-inch sliced
- ¾ of red bell pepper, sliced
- ½ of onion, peeled, sliced
- ½ of key lime, juiced
- 2 spelt flour tortillas
- Extra:
- 1/3 teaspoon salt
- ¼ teaspoon cayenne pepper
- ¼ teaspoon onion powder
- 1 tablespoon grapeseed oil

Directions

1. Take a medium skillet pan, place it over medium heat, add oil and when hot, add onion and red pepper, and then cook for 2 minutes until tender-crisp.

2. Add mushrooms slices, sprinkle with all the seasoning, stir until mixed, and then cook for 5 minutes until vegetables turn soft.
3. Heat the tortilla until warm, distribute vegetables in their center, drizzle with lime juice, and then roll tightly.
4. Storage instructions:
5. Cool the wraps, cover with a plastic wrap and then with foil, and then store in the refrigerator for up to 5 days.
6. Reheating instructions:
7. When ready to eat, reheat in the oven for 1 to 2 minutes until hot and then serve.

Nutrition: 337 Calories; 3.7 g Fats; 2.6 g Protein; 73.3 g Carbohydrates; 21.3 g Fiber;

140. **Grilled Watermelon**

Preparation Time: 10 minutes
Cooking Time: 4 minutes
Servings: 4
Ingredients:

- 1 watermelon, peeled and cut into 1-inch-thick wedges
- 1 garlic clove, minced finely
- 2 tablespoons fresh key lime juice
- Pinch of cayenne powder
- Pinch of sea salt

Directions:

1. Preheat the grill to high heat.
2. Grease the grill grate.
3. Place the watermelon pieces onto the grill and cook for about 2 minutes per side.
4. Meanwhile, in a bowl, mix together the remaining Ingredients:.
5. Drizzle the watermelon slices with garlic mixture and serve.

Nutrition: Calories 11 Fats 0 g Cholesterol 0 mg Carbohydrates 2.7 g Fiber 0.2 g Protein 0.2 g

141. **Avocado Gazpacho**

Preparation Time: 15 minutes
Cooking Time: 15 minutes
Servings: 6
Ingredients:

- 3 large avocados; peeled, pitted, and chopped
- 1/3 cup fresh cilantro leaves
- 3 cups spring water
- 2 tablespoons fresh key lime juice

- ¼ teaspoon cayenne powder
- Sea salt, as needed

Directions:
1. In a high-powered blender, put all Ingredients: and pulse until smooth.
2. Transfer the soup into a large bowl.
3. Cover the bowl of gazpacho and refrigerate to chill for at least 2–3 hours before serving.

Nutrition: Calories 206 Fats 4.1 g Cholesterol 0 mg Carbohydrates 8.8 g Fiber 6.8 g Protein 1.9 g

142. Mango Salsa

Preparation Time: 15 minutes
Cooking Time: 15 minutes
Servings: 6
Ingredients:
- 1 avocado; peeled, pitted, and cubed
- 2 tablespoons fresh key lime juice
- 1 mango; peeled, pitted, and cubed
- 1 cup cherry tomatoes, quartered
- 1 tablespoon fresh cilantro, chopped
- Sea salt, as needed

Directions:
1. In a bowl, add avocado cubes and lime juice and mix well.
2. In the bowl, add remaining Ingredients: and stir to combine.
3. Serve immediately.

Nutrition: Calories 108 Fats 1.4 g Cholesterol 0 mg Carbohydrates 12.5 g Fiber 3.5 g Protein 1.4 g

143. Banana Chips

Preparation Time: 10 minutes
Cooking Time: 1 hour
Servings: 6
Ingredients:
- 5 burro bananas, peeled and cut into ¼-inch-thick slices

Directions:
1. Preheat your oven to 250°F.
2. Line a large baking sheet with baking paper.
3. Place the banana slices onto the prepared baking sheet in a single layer.
4. Bake for approximately 1 hour.

Nutrition: Calories 88 Fats 0.1 g Cholesterol 0 mg Carbohydrates 22.5 g Fiber 2.6 g Protein 1.1 g

144. Chickpeas Fries

Preparation Time: 20 minutes
Cooking Time: 50 minutes
Servings: 8
Ingredients:
- 4 cups spring water
- 2 cups chickpea flour
- ½ cup green bell peppers, seeded and chopped
- ½ cup onions, chopped
- 1 tablespoon fresh oregano, chopped
- 1 teaspoon onion powder
- 1 teaspoon cayenne powder
- Sea salt, as needed

Directions:
1. Line a baking sheet with a greased parchment paper.
2. In a large pan, add the water and flour over medium heat and beat until well combined.
3. Add the remaining Ingredients: and cook for about 10 minutes, stirring frequently.
4. Remove from the heat and place the mixture onto the prepared baking sheet.
5. With a spatula, smooth the top surface.
6. With another lightly greased parchment paper, cover the surface and with another baking sheet, press tightly.
7. Freeze for about 20 minutes.
8. Preheat your oven to 400°F.
9. Lightly grease a baking sheet.
10. Remove the parchment paper from top and cut into desired-sized fries.
11. Arrange the fries onto the prepared baking sheet in a single layer.
12. Bake for approximately 20 minutes.
13. Carefully flip the fries over and bake for approximately 10–15 minutes.
14. Serve warm.

Nutrition: Calories 98 Fats 0.2 g Cholesterol 0 mg Carbohydrates 15.3 g Fiber 3.1 g Protein 5.4 g

145. Chilled Mango Treat

Preparation Time: 10 minutes
Cooking Time: 10 minutes
Servings: 4
Ingredients:
- 3 cups frozen mango; peeled, pitted, and chopped
- 1 tablespoon fresh mint leaves
- 2 tablespoons fresh key lime juice

- ½ cup chilled spring water

Directions:
1. In a high-powered blender, put all Ingredients: and pulse until smooth.
2. Transfer into serving bowls and serve immediately.

Nutrition: Calories 76 Fats 0.1 g Cholesterol 0 mg Carbohydrates 18.7 g Fiber 2.1 g Protein 1.1 g

146. Strawberry Ice Cream

Preparation Time: 15 minutes
Cooking Time: 15 minutes
Servings: 6
Ingredients:
- 5 frozen burro bananas
- 1 cup frozen strawberries
- ½ of avocado; peeled, pitted, and chopped
- ¼ cup unsweetened hemp milk
- 1 tablespoon agave nectar

Directions:
1. In a high-powered blender, put all Ingredients: and pulse until smooth.
2. Transfer the strawberry mixture into an airtight container and refrigerate for about 4–6 hours or until firm before serving.

Nutrition: Calories 143 Fats 0.8 g Cholesterol 0 mg Carbohydrates 28.5 g Fiber 4.3 g Protein 1.6 g

147. Lime Sorbet

Preparation Time: 10 minutes
Cooking Time: 10 minutes
Servings: 4
Ingredients:
- 2 tablespoons fresh key lime zest, grated
- ½ cup agave nectar
- 2 cups spring water
- 1½ cups fresh key lime juice

Directions:
1. Freeze ice cream maker tub for about 24 hours before making this sorbet.
2. In a non-stick saucepan, add all of the Ingredients: (except for lime juice) over medium heat and simmer for about 1 minute, stirring continuously.
3. Remove the pan of mixture from heat and stir in the lime juice.
4. Transfer this into an airtight container and refrigerate for about 2 hours.

5. Now, place the lime mixture into an ice cream maker and process it according to the manufacturer's directions.
6. Return the ice cream to the airtight container and freeze for about 2 hours.

Nutrition: Calories 130 Fats 0 g Cholesterol 0 mg Carbohydrates 33.4 g Fiber 2.3 g Protein 0.1 g

148. Avocado Mousse

Preparation Time: 15 minutes
Cooking Time: 15 minutes
Servings: 4
Ingredients:
- 2 cups burro bananas, peeled and chopped
- 2 ripe avocados; peeled, pitted, and chopped
- 2 teaspoons fresh key lime zest, grated finely
- 1 cup fresh key lime juice
- 1/3–½ cup agave nectar

Directions:
1. In a blender, put all Ingredients: and pulse on high speed until smooth and creamy.
2. Transfer the mousse into four serving glasses and refrigerate to chill for about 3 hours before serving.

Nutrition: Calories 358 Fats 4.2 g Cholesterol 281 mg Carbohydrates 47.9 g Fiber 10.1 g Protein 2.8 g

149. Grilled Peaches

Preparation Time: 10 minutes
Cooking Time: 6 minutes
Servings: 2
Ingredients:
- 2 large peaches, halved and pitted
- 1/8 teaspoon ground cinnamon
- 1 tablespoon walnuts, chopped

Directions:
1. Preheat the grill to medium-high heat.
2. Grease the grill grate.
3. Arrange the peach halves onto the prepared grill, cut side down and cook for about 3–5 minutes per side.
4. Remove the peach halves from grill and place onto serving plates.
5. Set aside to cool slightly.
6. Sprinkle with cinnamon and walnuts and serve.

Nutrition: Calories 83 Fats 0.1 g Cholesterol 0 mg Carbohydrates 14.5 g Fiber 2.6 g Protein 2.4 g

150. Pasta with Chickpea Sauce

Preparation Time: 10 minutes
Cooking Time: 10 minutes
Ingredients:
- ½ cup cooked chickpeas
- 2 cups cooked spelt pasta, hot
- ½ cup chopped onion
- 2 tablespoons chopped basil
- Extra:
- 1 ½ tablespoon olive oil
- 1/3 cup spring water
- ½ teaspoon salt
- ¼ teaspoon cayenne pepper

Directions:
1. Take a medium skillet pan, place it over medium heat, add oil and when hot, add onion, and cook for 5 to 8 minutes until golden brown.
2. Spoon the onion mixture into a food processor, add chickpeas, salt, cayenne pepper, and water and then pulse until smooth.
3. Place pasta into a large bowl, add blended chickpea sauce, toss until mixed, and then garnish with basil.

Nutrition: 197 Calories; 6.1 g Fats; 6 g Protein; 30.5 g Carbohydrates; 5 g Fiber;

151. Spiced Chickpeas

Preparation Time: 5 minutes
Cooking Time: 10 minutes
Ingredients:
- 1 ½ cup cooked chickpeas
- 8 cherry tomatoes, chopped
- 1 medium onion, peeled, sliced
- ¾ cup vegetable broth, homemade
- Extra:
- 6 teaspoons spice mix
- ¼ teaspoon salt
- ½ tablespoon grapeseed oil
- ¼ teaspoon cayenne pepper
- ¾ cup tomato sauce, alkaline
- 6 tablespoons soft-jelly coconut milk

Directions:
1. Take a large skillet pan, place it over medium heat, add oil and warm, add onion, and then cook for 5 minutes until golden brown.
2. Add spice mix, add remaining Ingredients: into the pan except for okra, stir until mixed, and then bring the mixture to a simmer.

3. Add chickpeas, stir until mixed, and then cook for 5 minutes over medium-low heat setting until thoroughly warmed.

Nutrition: 187.9 Calories; 7.7 g Fats; 6.4 g Protein; 26.2 g Carbohydrates; 6.6 g Fiber;
Carbohydrates; 1.8 g Fiber;

HERBAL TEA RECIPES

152. Liver-Kidney Cleansing Tea

Preparation Time: 5 minutes
Cooking Time: 0 minutes
Ingredients:
- 1 teaspoon dandelion root powder
- 1 teaspoon burdock root powder
- 1 cup spring water

Directions:
1. Place all Ingredients: in a tea kettle
2. Boil for 10 minutes, remove from heat, cover and leave for an additional 10 minutes.
3. Drain and serve

Nutrition: 120 Calories; 1.4 g Fats; 6 g Protein; 28 g Carbohydrates; 5 g Fiber;

153. Refreshing Kidney Cleansing tea

Preparation Time: 5 minutes
Cooking Time: 0 minutes
Serving: 1
Ingredients:
- 1 teaspoon Prodigiosa powder
- 1 teaspoon burdock root powder
- 1 cup spring water

Directions:
1. Place all Ingredients: in a tea kettle
2. Boil for 10 minutes, remove from heat, cover and leave for an additional 10 minutes.
3. Drain and serve

Nutrition: 132 Calories; 1.6 g Fats; 4 g Protein; 27 g

Carbohydrates; 3 g Fiber;

154. Mucus Liver Cleansing Tea

Preparation Time: 5 minutes
Cooking Time: 0 minutes
Serving: 1
Ingredients:
- 1 teaspoon dandelion root powder
- 1 teaspoon Prodigiosa powder
- 1 cup spring water

Directions:
1. Place all Ingredients: in a tea kettle
2. Boil for 10 minutes, remove from heat, cover and leave for an additional 10 minutes.
3. Drain and serve

Nutrition: 140 Calories; 1.5 g Fats; 4g Protein; 16 g Carbohydrates; 6 g Fiber;

155. Colon-Gallbladder Cleansing Tea

Preparation Time: 5 minutes
Cooking Time: 0 minutes
Serving: 1
Ingredients:
- 1 teaspoon Cascara powder
- 1 teaspoon Rhubard root powder
- 1 cup spring water

Directions:
1. Place all Ingredients: in a tea kettle
2. Boil for 10 minutes, remove from heat, cover and leave for an additional 10 minutes.
3. Drain and serve

Nutrition: 113 Calories; 1.5 g Fats; 6 g Protein; 22 g Carbohydrates; 3 g Fiber;

156. Colon-Gallbladder Tea

Preparation Time: 5 minutes
Cooking Time: 0 minutes
Serving: 2
Ingredients:
- 1 teaspoon Cascara powder
- 1 teaspoon Cahparral
- 1 cup spring water

Directions:
1. Place all Ingredients: in a tea kettle
2. Boil for 10 minutes, remove from heat, cover and leave for an additional 10 minutes.

3. Drain and serve

Nutrition: 130 Calories; 2.5 g Fats; 5 g Protein; 24 g Carbohydrates; 4 g Fiber;

157. Respiratory Mucus Cleansing tea

Preparation Time: 5 minutes
Cooking Time: 0 minutes
Serving: 1
Ingredients:
- 1 teaspoon Guaco herb
- 1 teaspoon Mullein
- 1 cup spring water

Directions:
1. Place all Ingredients: in a tea kettle
2. Boil for 10 minutes, remove from heat, cover and leave for an additional 10 minutes.
3. Drain and serve

Nutrition: 142 Calories; 1.8 g Fats; 4 g Protein; 28 g Carbohydrates; 6 g Fiber;

158. Respiratory and Mucus Syrup (Elderberry Syrup)

Preparation Time: 5 minutes
Cooking Time: 0 minutes
Service: 1
Ingredients:
- 1 teaspoon Elderberry fruit
- 1 cup spring water

Directions:
1. Place all Ingredients: in a tea kettle
2. Boil for 5 minutes, remove from heat, cover and leave for an additional 10 minutes.
3. Drain and serve

Nutrition: 124 Calories; 1.8 g Fats; 5 g Protein; 19 g Carbohydrates; 5 g Fiber;

159. Immune Boosting Tea

Preparation Time: 5 minutes
Cooking Time: 10 minutes
Serving: 1
Ingredients:
- 1 teaspoon linden powder
- 1 cup spring water

Directions:
1. Place all Ingredients: in a tea kettle

2. Boil for 5 minutes, remove from heat, cover and leave for an additional 10 minutes.
3. Drain and serve
4. **Nutrition:** 123 Calories; 1.5 g Fats; 4 g Protein; 17 g Carbohydrates; 4 g Fiber;

160. Bromide Plus Cleansing Drink

Preparation Time: 5 minutes
Cooking Time: 10 minutes
Serving: 1
Ingredients:
- 1 teaspoon bromide plus powder
- 1 teaspoon dandelion root powder
- 1 cup spring water

Directions:
1. Place all Ingredients: in a tea kettle
2. Boil for 10 minutes, remove from heat, cover and leave for an additional 10 minutes.
3. Drain and serve

Nutrition: 130 Calories; 1.4 g Fats; 5 g Protein; 27 g Carbohydrates; 4 g Fiber;

161. Bromide Plus Revitalizing Tea

Preparation Time: 5 minutes
Cooking Time: 0 minutes
Serving: 1
Ingredients:
- 1 teaspoon bromide plus powder
- Handful chamomile flowers
- 1 cup spring water

Directions:
1. Place flowers and water into a kettle.
2. Boil for 5 minutes, remove from heat, cover and leave for an additional 10 minutes.
3. Drain and add bromide powder.
4. Serve

Nutrition: 120 Calories; 2.5 g Fats; 6 g Protein; 27 g Carbohydrates; 5 g Fiber;

162. Respiratory Power Boost

Preparation Time: 5 minutes
Cooking Time: 10 minutes
Serving: 1
Ingredients:
- 1 teaspoon Guaco herb
- 1 teaspoon Mullein
- 1 cup spring water

Directions:
1. Place all Ingredients: in a tea kettle
2. Boil for 10 minutes, remove from heat, cover and leave for an additional 10 minutes.
3. Drain and serve

Nutrition: 110 Calories; 1.2 g Fats; 5 g Protein; 16 g Carbohydrates; 3 g Fiber;

163. Chamomile Herbal Tea

Preparation Time: 5 minutes
Cooking Time: 5 minutes
Servings: 2
Ingredients:
- 2 thin apple slices
- 2 cups boiling spring water
- 2 tablespoons fresh chamomile flowers, rinsed
- 1–2 teaspoons agave nectar

Directions:
1. Rinse the teapot with boiling water.
2. In the warm pot, place the apple slices and with a wooden spoon, mash them.
3. Add the chamomile flowers and top with the boiling water.
4. Cover the pot and steep for 3–5 minutes.
5. Strain the tea into two serving cups and stir in the agave nectar.
6. Serve immediately.

Nutrition: Calories 68 Fats 0g Cholesterol 0 mg Carbohydrates 18.1 g Fiber 2.9 g Protein 0.3 g

164. Burdock Herbal Tea

Preparation Time: 5 minutes
Cooking Time: 5 minutes
Servings: 2
Ingredients:
- 2 teaspoons dried burdock root
- 2 cups boiling spring water

Directions:
1. In a teapot, add the burdock root and top with the boiling water.
2. Cover the pot and steep for 3–5 minutes.
3. Strain the tea into two serving cups and serve immediately.

Nutrition: Calories 2 Fats 0 g Cholesterol 0 mg Carbohydrates 0.4 g Fiber 0.1 g Protein 0 g

165. Elderberry Herbal Tea

Preparation Time: 10 minutes
Cooking Time: 20 minutes
Servings: 2
Ingredients:
- 16 ounces spring water
- 2 tablespoons dried elderberries
- ½ teaspoon ground turmeric
- ¼ teaspoon ground cinnamon
- 1 teaspoon agave nectar

Directions:
1. In a small saucepan, place water and elderberries, turmeric and cinnamon over medium-high heat and bring to a boil.
2. Now, adjust the heat to low and simmer for about 15 minutes.
3. Remove from heat and set aside to cool for about 5 minutes.
4. Through a fine mesh strainer, strain the tea into serving cups and stir in the agave nectar.
5. Serve immediately.

Nutrition: Calories 19 Fats 0 g Cholesterol 0 mg Carbohydrates 4.9 g Fiber 1.1 g Protein 0.1 g

166. Fennel Herbal Tea

Preparation Time: 5 minutes
Cooking Time: 5 minutes
Servings: 2
Ingredients:
- 2–4 teaspoons fennel seeds, crushed freshly
- 2 cups boiling spring water

Directions:
1. In a teapot, add the fennel seeds and top with the boiling water.
2. Cover the pot and steep for 5–10 minutes.
3. Strain the tea into two serving cups and serve immediately.

Nutrition: Calories 7 Fats 0 g Cholesterol 0 mg Carbohydrates 1.1 g Fiber 0.8 g Protein 0.3 g

167. Fennel & Ginger Herbal Tea

Preparation Time: 10 minutes
Cooking Time: 5 minutes
Servings: 2
Ingredients:
- 2 cups spring water
- 1 tablespoon fennel seeds, crushed slightly

- 1 (½-inch) piece fresh ginger, peeled and crushed slightly
- 2 teaspoons agave nectar

Directions:
1. In a small saucepan, add water over medium heat and bring to a rolling boil.
2. Stir in the fennel seeds and ginger and remove from the heat.
3. Strain the tea into two serving cups and stir in the agave nectar.
4. Serve immediately.

Nutrition: Calories 33 Fats 0 g Cholesterol 0 mg Carbohydrates 7.5 g Fiber 1.6 g Protein 0.5 g

168. Ginger & Cinnamon Herbal Tea

Preparation Time: 10 minutes
Cooking Time: 10 minutes
Servings: 1
Ingredients:
- 1 cup spring water
- 1 (1-inch) piece fresh ginger, cut into pieces
- 1 cinnamon stick
- 1 teaspoon agave nectar

Directions:
1. In a saucepan, add water, ginger, and cinnamon over high heat and bring to a boil.
2. Now, adjust the heat to low and simmer for about 5 minutes.
3. Remove the saucepan of tea from the and strain into a serving cup.
4. Stir in the agave nectar and serve immediately.

Nutrition: Calories 40 Fats 0.1 g Cholesterol 0 mg Carbohydrates 9.6 g Fiber 1.3 g Protein 0.5 g

169. Ginger & Lime Herbal Tea

Preparation Time: 10 minutes
Cooking Time: 15 minutes
Servings: 2
Ingredients:
- 2 cups spring water
- 2 tablespoons fresh ginger root, cut into slices
- 1 tablespoon fresh key lime juice
- 1 tablespoon agave nectar

Directions:
1. In a saucepan, add water, ginger, and cinnamon over high heat and bring to a boil.

2. Now, adjust the heat to low and simmer for about 10 minutes.
3. Remove the saucepan of tea from the and strain into serving cups.
4. In the cups, stir in the lime juice and agave nectar and serve immediately.

Nutrition: Calories 34 Fats 0 g Cholesterol 0 mg Carbohydrates 8.6 g Fiber 0.6 g Protein 0.1 g

170. Linden Herbal Tea

Preparation Time: 5 minutes
Cooking Time: 6 minutes
Servings: 1
Ingredients:
- 2 teaspoon fresh linden flowers
- 1 cup spring water
- 1 teaspoon agave nectar

Directions:
1. In a saucepan, add water over medium heat and bring to a boil.
2. Stir in the linden flowers and cook for about 1 minute.
3. Remove from the heat and set aside, covered for about 10 minutes.
4. Strain the tea into a serving cup and stir in the agave nectar.
5. Serve immediately.

Nutrition: Calories 20 Fats 0 g Cholesterol 0 mg Carbohydrates 5.3 g Fiber 0.3 g Protein 0 g

171. Raspberry Herbal Tea

Preparation Time: 5 minutes
Cooking Time: 5 minutes
Servings: 1
Ingredients:
- 1–2 teaspoons red raspberry leaf tea
- 1 cup boiling spring water
- 1 teaspoon agave nectar

Directions:
1. In the teapot, place the raspberry leaf tea and top with the boiling water.
2. Cover the pot and steep for 3–5 minutes.
3. Strain the tea into two serving cups and stir in the agave nectar.
4. Serve immediately.

Nutrition: Calories 20 Fats 0 g Cholesterol 0 mg Carbohydrates 5.3 g Fiber 0.3 g Protein 0 g

172. Anise & Cinnamon Herbal Tea

Preparation Time: 5 minutes
Cooking Time: 15 minutes
Servings: 2

Ingredients:

- 7 star anise
- 1 (2-inch) cinnamon stick
- 2–3 cups water

Directions:

1. In a saucepan, add water over medium heat and bring to a rolling boil.
2. Add star anise and cinnamon stick and boil for about 10 minutes.
3. Remove from heat and steep, covered for about 3 minutes.
4. Strain the tea into two serving cups and stir in the agave nectar.
5. Serve immediately.

Nutrition: Calories 20 Fats 0 g Cholesterol 0 mg Carbohydrates 4.4 g Fiber 2.3 g Protein 0.7 g

ALKALINE DIET RECIPES

173. Alkaline Vegan Pink Smoothie

Preparation Time: 5 minutes
Cooking Time: 0 minutes
Serving: 2
Ingredients:
- 1 burro banana, peeled
- ½ cup raspberries
- 1 mango, peeled, destoned, diced
- ½ cup walnut milk, homemade

Directions:
1. Plug in a high-speed food processor or blender and add all the Ingredients: in its jar.
2. Cover the blender jar with its lid and then pulse for 40 to 60 seconds until smooth.
3. Divide the drink between two glasses and then serve.

Nutrition: 222.7 Calories; 2.2 g Fats; 4.6 g Protein; 50.3 g Carbohydrates; 7.3 g Fiber;

174. Alkalizing Green Soup

Preparation Time: 10 minutes
Cooking Time: 10 minutes
Servings: 2
Ingredients:
- 1 tablespoon sunflower or coconut oil
- 1 pint of stock made with 1 tablespoon vegetable Bouillon powder
- 1/4 tablespoon fennel seeds
- ½ red onion- finely chopped

- 1 cup tender stem broccoli
- 1¼ cups baby spinach
- Juice and zest of 1 lemon
- 1 clove garlic- finely chopped

Directions:
1. Fry the garlic, red onions, and fennel seeds in oil over medium heat for about 2 minutes.
2. Add in the broccoli, zest, stock, and lemon juice and let it cook for 4 minutes.
3. Pull out from heat and toss in the baby spinach. Stir until the spinach is wilted.
4. Immediately add the mixture to a blender and blend until smooth.
5. **Nutrition:** Calories 132 Fat 8g, Fiber 2g, Carbohydrates 8g, Protein 8

175. Alkaline Cauliflower Fried Rice

Preparation Time: 5 minutes
Cooking Time: 5 minutes
Servings: 4
Ingredients:
- 1 zucchini (courgette)
- 1 inch fresh root ginger
- 1 inch fresh root turmeric
- 1 large cauliflower
- 1/2 bunch of kale (any variety)
- 1 tablespoon coconut oil
- 1 bunch of coriander
- 1/2 bunch parsley (any variety)
- 1 bunch mint
- 1 tablespoon tamari soy sauce or bragg liquid aminos
- 1 lime
- 4 spring onions
- 2 handfuls almonds
- Optional
- 1 green chili
- Instead of ginger and fresh turmeric, use 1 teaspoon of each powdered

Directions:
1. Begin by making the rice of cauliflower–it's very easy–just split the cauli into small florets and chop it into your blender or food processor and pulse until it's like rice. Unless you don't have the blender, you can only grate it and get an effect that is very close.
2. Now is veggie preparation Time, so thinly slice your kale, quarter and then thinly slice the courgette

(zucchini) and chop all your herbs roughly (discard the basil and parsley stems, but keep the coriander stems) next, prepare your ginger and turmeric—first by peeling them (for quick peeling, just scrape back of a spoon over the ginger/turmeric—sweet!) And then rub them in a big bowl.

3. Stir the coriander into the mix including the stems as this begins warming up.
4. Stir in the cauliflower after 30 seconds and then the kale after another 2 min-3 minutes, add the spring onions and then the rest of the herbs, the bragg/tamari and stir through—and then remove from the heat—the total cooking Time will be less than 5 minutes—you don't want it to go too soft!
5. Now chop and mix the almonds roughly, season to taste, and add lime juice according to your favorite.

Nutrition: Calories: 109.5 Fat: 7.5g Cholesterol: 93.5g Carbohydrates: 6.8g Protein: 5.3g

176. Alkaline Mushroom Chickpea Burgers Recipe

Preparation Time: 20 minutes
Cooking Time: 30 minutes
Servings: 8
Ingredients:

- 2 portobello mushrooms
- 2 cups cooked chickpeas
- 2 tablespoons Onion powder
- 2 tablespoons Himalayan sea salt
- 2 tablespoons Oregano
- 1/2 cup cilantro
- 1/4 cup garbanzo bean flour
- 1/2 tablespoon. Cayenne
- 1/2 cup green peppers
- 1/2 cup red and white onions
- Food processor or blender
- 1/4 measurement cup

Directions:

1. Chop the mushrooms into chunks and dice the vegetables.
2. Place all the ingredients in a food processor and pulse for 3 seconds.
3. Check for consistency, if it's too wet, add more flour then scoop into a bowl.
4. Set your cooker to medium heat and sprinkle grapeseed oil into the skillet.
5. Scoop the blend into a cup and turn it over to your cooking surface.

6. Allow the blend to for 5 minutes on each side. Apply caution when flipping so that the blend can stay together.
7. Your alkaline mushroom/chickpea burgers are ready to be served.

Nutrition: Calories: 225 Carbohydrates: 22.5g Fat: 14.2g Protein: 11.4g

177. Alkaline Veggie Fajitas Recipe

Preparation Time: 10 minutes
Cooking Time: 20 minutes
Servings: 6-12
Ingredients:

- 1/2 cups cut green and red peppers
- 1/2 cups cut red and white onions
- 3 cups cut mushrooms
- 2 tablespoon Ocean salt
- 2 tablespoon Onion powder
- 2 tablespoon Sweet basil
- 2 tablespoon Oregano
- 1/2 tablespoon Cayenne powder
- Juice from 1/2 of a lime
- Grapeseed oil
- Alkaline spelt tortillas
- Alkaline guacamole (discretionary)
- Alkaline mango salsa (discretionary)
- If you would prefer not to utilize mushrooms in this formula, you can essentially preclude them and cut each preparing down the middle

Directions:

1. Make your mushrooms, bell peppers, and onions into long strips.
2. Set your cooker to medium heat then sprinkle a tablespoon of grapeseed oil on the skillet.
3. Sprinkle another tablespoon of grapeseed oil on a large skillet.
4. Mix your vegetables and seasoning, then, sauté for 5 minutes.
5. Serve them on spelt tortillas with the guacamole and salsa.
6. Your alkaline veggie fajitas are ready to be dished.

Nutrition: Calories: 257 Fat: 2g Protein: 12.9g Carbohydrates: 50.3g

178. Alkaline Roasted Tomato Sauce Recipe

Preparation Time: 15 minutes

Cooking Time: 40 minutes
Servings: 6
Ingredients:
- 18 Roma tomatoes
- 1/2 red bell pepper
- 1/2 sweet onion
- 1/2 red onion
- 1 medium shallot
- 1/8 cup grapeseed oil
- 1 tablespoon agave
- 3 teaspoons sea salt
- 3 teaspoons basil
- 2 teaspoons oregano
- 2 teaspoons onion powder
- 1/8 teaspoon cayenne powder
- Equipment
- Blender
- Cookie sheet
- Parchment paper
- Pot—at least 4 quart

Directions:
1. Preheat your oven to 400° f.
2. Chop the vegetables in half and place them in a bowl.
3. Sprinkle grapeseed oil and a teaspoon of both basil and sea salt.
4. Sprinkle the chopped vegetables in the mixture until it is fully coated.
5. Place all the vegetables on a cookie sheet.
6. Bake in the oven for 30 minutes.
7. Toss the roasted vegetables into a blender and blend on high speed.
8. Pour the pasta and the remaining ingredients into a pot. Allow it to cook for 20 minutes.

Nutrition: Calories: 25 Fat: 2g Sodium: 80mg Carbohydrates: 2g

179. Alkaline Vegan Hot Dogs Recipe

Preparation Time: 20 minutes
Cooking Time: 40 minutes
Servings: 10
Ingredients:
- 1 cup garbanzo beans
- 1 cup spelt flour
- 1/2 cup aquafaba
- 1/3 cup green pepper, diced
- 1/3 cup onion, diced
- 1/4 cup shallots, diced
- 1 tablespoon Onion powder
- 2 tablespoon Smoked sea salt
- 1 tablespoon Coriander
- 1/2 tablespoon Ginger
- 1/2 tablespoon Dill
- 1/2 tablespoon Fennel
- 1/2 tablespoon Crushed red pepper (optional)
- Alkaline electric ketchup (optional)
- Grapeseed oil for sautéing
- Alkaline electric buns (optional)
- When trying to make hotdog buns, all you have to do is follow the recipe to roll the dough then bake on a taco rack. In the absence of a rack, flatbread or tortillas can be used instead.
- Tools:
- Hotdog mold
- Food processor
- Parchment paper
- Taco rack (optional)

Directions:
1. Sprinkle grapeseed oil in your skillet, add vegetables and garbanzo beans then sauté for 5 minutes.
2. Place the remaining vegetables and other ingredients in a food processor until it is well blended.
3. Scoop the mixture into your hand, then, make hotdog shapes with them and wrap with parchment paper afterward.
4. The molded hotdogs should be steamed for 40 minutes.
5. Once the steaming process is done, unwrap the hotdogs.
6. Sprinkle grapeseed oil in a skillet and cook the hotdogs for 10 minutes on medium heat.
7. Your alkaline electric hotdogs are ready to be dished.

Nutrition: Calories: 159.2 Carbohydrates: 6.3g Fat: 3.3g Protein: 25.5g

180. Alkaline Avocado Mayo Recipe

Preparation Time: 10 minutes
Cooking Time: 10 minutes
Servings: 1 cup
Ingredients:
- Juice from half of a lime
- 1 avocado

- 1/4 cup cilantro
- 1/2 tablespoon Sea salt
- 1/2 tablespoon Onion powder
- 2-4 tablespoon Olive oil
- Pinch of cayenne powder
- Blender or hand mixer

Directions:
1. Remove the pit of the avocado and scoop the insides into a blender.
2. Add the rest of the ingredients and blend at a high speed.
3. For hand mixers, add all other ingredients except the oil which should be added slowly until the desired consistency is reached.
4. Dish your alkaline avocado mayo!

Nutrition: Calories: 45 Fat: 4.5g Sodium: 100mg Carbohydrates: 0.5g

181. Alkaline Quinoa Milk Recipe

Preparation Time: 10 minutes
Cooking Time: 5 minutes
Servings: 4
Ingredients:
- 1 cup cooked white quinoa
- 3 cups spring water
- 6-8 dates
- 1 pinch sea salt (optional)
- 1 pinch cloves (optional)
- Blender
- Milk bag or cheesecloth

Directions:
1. Make a perfect blend of these ingredients in a blender.
2. Sieve with milk bag or cheesecloth.
3. Enjoy your well-deserved alkaline quinoa milk recipe.

Nutrition: Calories: 111 Fat: 1.6g Carbohydrates: 20.7g Fiber: 2.3g

182. Alkaline Spicy Kale Recipe

Preparation Time: 10 minutes
Cooking Time: 15 minutes
Servings: 4
Ingredients:
- 1 bunch of kale
- 1/4 cup onion, diced
- 1/4 cup red pepper, diced

- 1 tablespoon Crushed red pepper
- 1/4 tablespoon Sea salt
- Alkaline "garlic" oil or grapeseed oil
- Salad spinner (optional)
- Note: if you happen to not have a salad spinner, you can as well air dry the kale.

Directions:
1. Rinse the kale, fold its leaves into halves, and cut off the stem.
2. Chop kale into bits and remove the water using a salad spinner.
3. Set your cooker to high and add 2 tablespoons of oil.
4. Sauté salt, pepper, and onions for 3 minutes.
5. Reduce the heat to low, add the chopped kale and cover for 5 minutes.
6. Crushed pepper should be introduced to the mix, stir and cover for another 3 minutes.
7. Dish your alkaline spicy kale!

Nutrition: Calories: 85.2 Fat: 1.2g Sodium: 61.2mg Carbohydrates: 18g Fiber: 5.9g Protein: 5.3g

183. Alkaline Buns Recipe

Preparation Time: 20 minutes
Cooking Time: 1 hour
Servings: 6
Ingredients:
- 2 1/4 cups - 2 1/2 cups spelt flour
- 1/2 cup hemp milk or walnut milk
- 1/4 cup aquafaba
- 1/4 cup sparkling spring water
- 1 tablespoon Agave
- 1 tablespoon Onion powder
- 1 1/2 tablespoon Sea salt
- 1 tablespoon Basil or oregano
- 2 tablespoon Grapeseed oil
- 1 tablespoon Sea moss gel (optional)
- Sesame seeds (optional)
- Baking sheet
- Plastic wrap
- Parchment paper
- Note: Mixer with a dough hook, if you do not have a mixer, you can knead by hand.

Directions:
1. Add all the dry ingredients into a mixing bowl and blend perfectly.

2. Add the remaining ingredients and blend on low speed for a minute. Then, knead dough at medium speed for 5 minutes.
3. Sprinkle grapeseed oil on a baking sheet already laced with parchment paper.
4. Separate dough into parts, roll with hand to make shapes then place on a baking sheet.
5. Brush the top with oil then add sesame seeds.
6. Use a plastic wrap to cover the buns and allow it to sit for 30 minutes.
7. Set your oven to 350°f and bake for half an hour.
8. Allow the buns to cook and carefully cut them in half to enjoy your alkaline electric buns!

Nutrition: Carbohydrates: 47g Fat: 7g Protein: 9g

184. Alkaline Strawberry Jam Recipe

Preparation Time: 10 minutes
Cooking Time: 20 minutes
Servings: 16 oz
Ingredients:
- 4 cups sliced strawberries
- 2/3 cups of raw agave
- 3 tablespoons of key lime juice
- 1/2 cup Irish moss gel

Directions:
1. Slice enough strawberries to fill up 4 cups.
2. Mash or blend to your desired texture.
3. Agave, lime juice, and strawberries should be added to the saucepan on high heat.
4. Cook for 10 minutes then add Irish moss gel.
5. Cook for 5 more minutes to make certain that the gel has been thoroughly dissolved.
6. Remove from heat and allow the sauce to cool down before refrigerating.
7. Dish your alkaline electric strawberry jam!

Nutrition: Calories: 56 Carbohydrates: 13g

185. Alkaline Date Syrup Recipe

Preparation Time: 10 minutes
Cooking Time: 15 minutes
Servings: 16-24 oz
Ingredients:
- 1 cup dates, preferably pitted
- 1 cup of spring water
- This sweetener can be easily dissolved in water, unlike date sugar.

Directions:
1. Boil spring water then remove from heat when boiled.

2. Place dates in the boiled water for at least 5 minutes.
3. Pour the dates and some water into a blender then blend for until it's smooth.
4. If the texture is too thick, add more water and blend again.
5. Keep it a refrigerator and dish with alkaline date syrup!

Nutrition: Calories: 270 Potassium: 848mg Sodium: 5mg Carbohydrates: 67g Fiber: 3g Sugar: 61g Protein: 1g

186. Alkaline Spaghetti Squash Recipe

Preparation Time: 10 minutes
Cooking Time: 30 minutes
Servings: 4
Ingredients:
- 1 spaghetti squash
- Grapeseed oil
- Sea salt
- Cayenne powder (optional)
- Onion powder (optional)

Directions:
1. Preheat your oven to 375°f
2. Carefully chop off the ends of the squash and cut it in half.
3. Scoop out the seeds into a bowl.
4. Coat the squash with oil.
5. Season the squash and flip it over for the other side to get baked. When properly baked, the outside of the squash will be tender.
6. Allow the squash to cool off, then, use a fork to scrape the inside into a bowl.
7. Add seasoning to taste.
8. Dish your alkaline spaghetti squash!

Nutrition: Calories: 672 Carbohydrates: 65g Fat: 47g Protein: 12g

187. Creamy Banana Pie Alkaline

Preparation Time: 10 minutes
Cooking Time: 2 hours
Servings: 4
Ingredients:
- Pie Mixture
- 7 oz. of Creamed Coconut
- 1/8 tsp. of Sea Salt
- 1 cup of hemp milk
- 6 – 8 Baby/Burro Bananas

- 3 – 4 tbsp. of Agave
- Crust
- 1/4 tsp. of Sea Salt
- 1 1/2 cups Coconut Chips / Flakes Unsweetened
- 1 1/2 cups pitted Dates,
- 1/4 cup of Agave
- Equipment
- Pie Dish
- Hand Mixer
- Food Processor

Directions:
1. Put all crust components in a blender & combine for 20 to 30 seconds till a ball is created.
2. Top spring-form pot with the waxed sheet, then thinly spread the crust mixture out.
3. In a spring-form container, put thin slices of banana across them, then store them in the freezer.
4. Apply the pie blend components to a big bowl and combine until well mixed with your mixer.
5. Pour the pie mixture over the spring-form bowl, shake the sides and then cover it with foil & enable it to freeze for about 3-4 hours.
6. Cover over coconut flakes, remove from the plate, and savor your Banana Pie!

Nutrition: Calories 224, Fat 12, Fiber 5, Carbohydrates 15, Protein 5

188. Ginger Shot Alkaline

Preparation Time: 10 minutes
Cooking Time: 10 minutes
Servings: 2
Ingredients:
- 1 apple small
- 2 ounces ginger root fresh
- Equipment
- Juice extractor

Directions:
1. Using a grater or spoon to scrape the ginger skin
2. Cut & add to the extractor for juice
3. Slice the apple and apply the ginger bits.
4. Juice
5. Add sliced apple & ginger to the mixer if you are using a processor.
6. Integrate 1-2 cups spring water
7. Mix well
8. Shear from a bag of cheesecloth or almond milk bag
9. Cherish the juice
10. P. S. As in spicy, this will be strongly intense & hot!

Nutrition: Calories 450, Fat 8g, Fiber 22g, Carbohydrates 8g, Protein 43g

189. Alkaline Raw Tahini Butter

Preparation Time: 10 minutes
Cooking Time: 5 minutes
Servings: 2
Ingredients:
- 1 – 2 tbsp of grape seed oil
- Sesame seeds raw
- Equipment
- Food processor or blender

Directions:
1. To a processor cup, apply pure sesame seeds
2. Mix so that the paste is chunky.
3. Add oil
4. Mix with the honey.
5. Store in the fridge in glass jars

Nutrition: Calories 555, Fat 28g, Fiber 2g, Carbohydrates 6g, Protein 67g

190. Alkaline Walnut Butter

Preparation Time: 10 minutes
Cooking Time: 10 minutes
Servings: 2
Ingredients:
- 1 tbsp raw agave (optional)
- 2 cups walnuts soaked
- 1/2 tsp sea salt
- 1 tsp avocado oil (optional)

Directions:
1. For a minimum of 1 hour or nightly, drench 2 cups of walnuts in the spring water.
2. Water dump and dispose of.
3. To produce a roasted taste, bake the nuts in the oven at 350 ° for about 10 minutes; this process is optional.
4. In a food processor, incorporate the nuts and combine until smooth, incorporating the rest of the materials.
5. Offer with spelt crackers or fruit

Nutrition: Calories 200, Fat 8g, Fiber 2g, Carbohydrates 8g, Protein 6g

191. Alkaline Applesauce

Preparation Time: 5 minutes
Cooking Time: 10 minutes

Servings: 2
Ingredients:
- 3 tbsp agave
- 1/8 tsp cloves
- 3 cups apples peeled, chopped
- 1 tsp of Seamoss gel
- 1 tsp lime juice
- 1/2 cup of strawberries
- 1/8 tsp sea salt
- Spring water
- Equipment
- Blender

Directions:
1. In addition to cloves, salt, lime juice, & agave, apply sliced apples to the blender.
2. Pulse to obtain the optimal quality using the blender.
3. Pulse through the strawberries just until combined.
4. If it doesn't mix well, apply 1 tablespoon of spring water.
5. Serving and relax! Preserve the leftover food in the freezer.

Nutrition: Calories 294, Fat 12g, Fiber 2g, Carbohydrates 8g, Protein 45g

192. **Alkaline Brazilian nut Cheesecake**

Preparation Time: 15 minutes
Cooking Time: 3 hours
Servings: 2
Ingredients:
- Cheesecake Mixture:
- 1/4 tsp. of Sea Salt
- 5-6 Dates
- 2 cups of Brazil Nuts
- 1/4 cup of Agave
- 1 1/2 cups Walnut Milk or Hemp Milk
- 1 tbsp. Gel of sea moss
- 2 tbsp. of lime Juice
- Crust:
- 1/4 tsp. of Sea Salt
- 1/4 cup of Agave
- 1 1/2 cups of Coconut Flakes
- 1 1/2 cups of Dates
- Toppings:
- Sliced Strawberries,
- Blackberries
- Sliced Raspberries,
- Sliced mango,
- Blueberries
- Equipment:
- Parchment Paper
- Blender
- Food Processor
- 8-inch Pan spring-form

Directions:
1. Put all the crust items and process for 20 seconds in the food processor.
2. In a springform pan filled with parchment, spread the crust out.
3. Place the thin slices of mango around the pan's corners and stay in the freezer.
4. Apply all the Ingredients: in the cheesecake blend to the blender and process until blend.
5. Pour the mixture over the crust, wrap in foil & allow 3-4 hours to settle.
6. Remove the pan's shape, layer your toppings &
7. Ensuring the leftovers are put in the fridge!

Nutrition: Calories 540, Fat 8g, Fiber 2g, Carbohydrates 8g, Protein 67g

193. **Alkaline Ginger Soup**

Preparation Time: 10 minutes
Cooking Time: 40 minutes
Servings: 2
Ingredients:
- 1 cup red peppers diced
- 12-16 cups of spring water
- 4-6 Leaves of Soursop
- 3 tbsp onion powder
- 2 cups kale chopped
- 1 cup onions diced
- 1 cup cubed zucchini
- 4 tsp sea salt
- 1 cup cubed summer squash
- 1 cup green peppers diced
- 1 tbsp minced fresh ginger,
- 2 cups cubed chayote squash
- 1 tbsp basil
- 1 cup Quinoa
- 1/4 tsp cayenne (optional)
- 1 tbsp oregano

Directions:
1. Rinse the leaves, rip them in half, and put them in a wide stockpot containing 4 cups of spring water.

2. With a cap on the kettle, boil the leaves for about 15-20 minutes.
3. Extract the leaves from the broth.
4. The remaining Ingredients: are added.
5. Add 8 cups of spring water.
6. Combine all the Ingredients:, replace the cap, and simmer for 30-45 minutes over medium heat. (If you do not use quinoa, more Time will be required.)

Nutrition: Calories 90, Fat 4g, Fiber 2g, Carbohydrates 8g, Protein 6g

ADDITIONAL RECIPES

194. Alkaline Zucchini Bacon

Preparation Time: 10 minutes
Cooking Time: 30 minutes
Servings: 2
Ingredients:

- 2 tbsp. of Agave
- 1/4 cup of Date
- 2-3 Zucchini
- 1 tbsp. of Sea Salt Smoked
- 1/2 tsp. of Cayenne Powder
- 1 tbsp. of Onion Powder
- 1/4 cup of Spring Water
- 1 tsp. of Liquid Smoke
- Grapeseed Oil
- 1/2 tsp. of Ginger Powder
- Equipment:
- Potato Peeler/ Mandoline
- Parchment Paper

Directions:

1. In a saucepan, incorporate all the Ingredients: and simmer on low heat until they are dissolved.
2. Chop finishes off the zucchini and makes strips with a potato peeler.
3. Toss the zucchini with the saucepan Ingredients: in a wide cup, then enable it to marinate for 30-60 minutes. There is no need for more water since it will emerge from zucchini.
4. On a baking sheet, put parchment paper and then brush lightly with the grapeseed oil.

5. Cover the marinated strips with the baking sheets, then bake at 400 ° F for 10 minutes.
6. Flip the strips of zucchini over & cook for the next 3-4 minutes, then let it cool off.
7. Cook for another few minutes or sear in a finely oil-coated pan for 30 seconds if you like to make any of the strips crispier.
8. Enjoy your Bacon with Zucchini!

Nutrition: Calories 200, Fat 8g, Fiber 2g, Carbohydrates 8g, Protein 6g

195. Alkaline Biscuits

Preparation Time: 10 minutes
Cooking Time: 20 minutes
Servings: 2
Ingredients:

- 1 tsp. of Sea Salt
- 3/4 cup Coconut Milk/Quinoa Milk
- 1/4 cup of Grapeseed Oil
- 2 cups of Spelt Flour
- Equipment:
- Cup/Cookie Cutter

Directions:

1. Mix all the components in a bowl together before they have shaped together into a ball.
2. Stretch out 1" thick dough, then turn the dough over the highest part of itself & spread out once again.
3. Slice out the biscuits using a cookie cutter after turning over the dough around 4-5 Times.
4. On a baking sheet, place the biscuits. (Optional parchment paper)
5. Bake about 18-20 minutes at 350 ° F.
6. Enable it to cool down and have fun.

Nutrition: Calories 120, Fat 8g, Fiber 2g, Carbohydrates 12g, Protein 3g

196. Alkaline Teff Sausage

Preparation Time: 10 minutes
Cooking Time: 10 minutes
Servings: 2
Ingredients:

- 1/4 cup onions diced
- 1 1/2 cups Teff Grain cooked
- 1 tbsp. diced Red Peppers,
- 2 tsp. of Ground Sage
- 1 tbsp. diced Green Peppers,
- 1 tsp. of Oregano

- 1/2 cup of Chickpea Flour
- 1 tbsp. of Onion Powder
- 1/2 tsp. of Dill
- 1 tsp. of Fennel Powder
- 1/2 tsp. Red Pepper Crushed
- 1 tsp. of Sea Salt
- 1 tsp. of Basil
- Grape seed Oil
- Equipment:
- Skillet
- Mixing Bowl

Directions:
1. Sauté the peppers & onions in around 1 tbsp of grapeseed oil for about 2-3 minutes over medium-high flame.
2. Lastly, apply the rest of the Ingredients: & sautéed veggies to chickpea flour in a wide bowl and combine well.
3. Add 1-2 teaspoons grapeseed oil to the skillet over medium heat.
4. Shape the teff blend forming patties & cook it on each side for 3 minutes until crunchy.
5. Cherish your sausage of Teff!

Nutrition: Calories 210g, Fat 12g, Fiber 2g, Carbohydrates 8g, Protein 6g

197. Alkaline French toast

Preparation Time: 10 minutes
Cooking Time: 20 minutes
Servings: 2
Ingredients:
- 1/2 cup Flour Garbanzo Bean
- Grapeseed Oil
- 1/2 tsp. of Ground Cloves
- 3/4 cup Walnut Milk /Hemp Milk
- 1/4 cup of Spring Water
- Spelt Bread
- 2 tbsp. of Agave
- 1/4 tsp. of Sea Salt
- Strawberries sliced (optional)
- 1/4 tsp. of Ginger Powder

Directions:
1. In a wide container, blend together all the Ingredients: until well combined.
2. Pour the batter into the long jar and allow the bread to steep for about 5-10 minutes, midway through tossing the bread.

3. Lightly oil the skillet using grape seed oil on a moderate flame and steam for about 3-4 minutes or till brown.
4. Round off with agave and strawberries and

Nutrition: Calories 170, Fat 8g, Fiber 2g, Carbohydrates 8g, Protein 4g

198. Alkaline Salad Burritos

Preparation Time: 10 minutes
Cooking Time: 5 minutes
Ingredients:
- 2 ounces arugula
- ¼ cup cherry tomatoes
- 2 tablespoons tahini butter, homemade
- ¾ cup cooked chickpeas
- 2 Kamut flour tortillas
- Extra:
- 1 tablespoon key lime juice
- ¼ teaspoon salt
- ¼ teaspoon cayenne pepper

Directions:
1. Prepare the dressing and for this, take a small bowl, place tahini butter in it and then stir in lime juice until mixed.
2. Take a medium bowl, place tomatoes in it, add arugula and chickpeas, drizzle with the dressing, toss until mixed, then cover the bowl and let it rest in the refrigerator for 20 minutes.
3. When ready to eat, heat the tortillas until warm, fill them with chickpeas mixture, sprinkle with salt and cayenne pepper, and then roll to serve.

Nutrition: 274 Calories; 9.1 g Fats; 11.5 g Protein; 39 g Carbohydrates; 4.4 g Fiber;

199. Alkaline Peach Muffin

Preparation Time: 10 minutes
Cooking Time: 15 minutes
Ingredients:
- 2/3 cup spelt flour
- ½ of peach, chopped
- 1 teaspoon mashed burro banana
- 2/3 tablespoons chopped walnuts
- 6 ½ tablespoons walnut milk, homemade
- Extra:
- 1/16 teaspoon salt
- 2 2/3 tablespoon date
- 2/3 tablespoon spring water, warmed

- 2/3 teaspoon key lime juice

Directions:
1. Switch on the oven, then set it to 400 degrees F and let it preheat.
2. Meanwhile, peel the peach, cut it in half, remove the pit and then cut one half of peach in ½-inch pieces, reserving the other half of peach for later use.
3. Take a medium bowl, pour in the milk, and then whisk in mashed burro banana and lime juice until well combined.
4. Take a separate medium bowl, place flour in it, add salt and date
5. , stir until mixed, whisk in milk mixture until smooth, and then fold in peached until mixed.
6. Take four silicone muffin cups, grease them with oil, fill them evenly with the prepared batter and then sprinkle walnuts on top.
7. Bake the muffins for 10 to 15 minutes until the top is nicely golden brown and inserted toothpick into each muffin comes out clean.
8. When done, let muffins cool for 10 minutes and then serve.

Nutrition: 76.1 Calories; 3.3 g Fats; 0.9 g Protein; 14.3 g Carbohydrates; 0.9 g Fiber;

200. Amaranth Porridge

Preparation Time: 10 minutes
Cooking Time: 25 minutes
Servings: 2
Ingredients:
1. 2 cups spring water
2. 2/3 cup amaranth
3. Pinch of sea salt
4. 1/3 cup unsweetened coconut milk
5. 2 teaspoons agave nectar
6. 2 tablespoons fresh blueberries

Directions:
1. In a small pan, place the water, amaranth, and salt over medium-high heat and bring to a rolling boil.
2. Now, adjust the heat to low and simmer, covered for about 20–25 minutes or until the amaranth has thickened, stirring twice.
3. Stir in the coconut milk and agave nectar and remove from the heat.
4. Serve hot with the topping of blueberries.

Nutrition: Calories 276 Fats 1.8 g Cholesterol 0 mg Carbohydrates 50 g Fiber 6.8 g Protein 9.5 g

201. Teff Porridge

Preparation Time: 10 minutes
Cooking Time: 20 minutes
Servings: 2
Ingredients:
- 2 cups spring water
- ½ cup teff grain
- Pinch of sea salt
- 1 tablespoon agave nectar
- 1 tablespoon walnuts, chopped

Directions:
1. In a small pan, place the water and salt over medium-high heat and bring to a boil.
2. Slowly, add the teff grain, stirring continuously.
3. Now, adjust the heat to low and cook, covered for about 15 minutes or until the amaranth has thickened, stirring twice.
4. Stir in the agave nectar and remove from the heat.
5. Serve hot with the topping of walnuts.

Nutrition: Calories 215 Fats 0.1 g Cholesterol 0 mg Carbohydrates 41.4 g Fiber 6.8 g Protein 6.9 g

202. Quinoa Porridge

Preparation Time: 15 minutes
Cooking Time: 24 minutes
Servings: 4
Ingredients:
- 1 cup uncooked quinoa, rinsed and drained
- 1 cup homemade walnut milk
- 1 cup unsweetened coconut milk
- Pinch of sea salt
- 2 tablespoons agave nectar
- ½ cup fresh strawberries, hulled and sliced

Directions:
1. Heat a non-stick saucepan over medium heat and cook the quinoa for about 3 minutes or until toasted slightly, stirring frequently.
2. Add the walnut milk, coconut milk, and a pinch of salt and stir to combine.
3. Now, adjust the heat to high and bring to a boil.
4. Reduce heat to low and cook, uncovered for about 20–25 minutes or until all the liquid is absorbed, stirring occasionally.
5. Remove the saucepan of quinoa from the heat and immediately, stir in the agave nectar.
6. Serve immediately with the topping of strawberry slices.

Nutrition: Calories 121 Fats 0.4 g Cholesterol 0 mg

Carbohydrates 18.8 g Fiber 4.2 g Protein 6.1 g

203. **Tomato Omelet**

Preparation Time: 10 minutes
Cooking Time: 30 minutes
Servings: 4
Ingredients:
- 1 cup chickpea flour
- ¼ teaspoon cayenne powder
- Pinch of ground cumin
- Pinch of sea salt
- 1½–2 cups spring water
- 1 medium onion, chopped finely
- 2 medium plum tomatoes, chopped finely
- 2 tablespoons fresh cilantro, chopped
- 2 tablespoons avocado oil, divided

Directions:
1. In a bowl, add the flour, spices, and salt and mix well.
2. Slowly, add the water and mix until well combined.
3. Fold in the onion, tomatoes, green chili, and cilantro.
4. In a large non-stick frying pan, heat ½ tablespoon of the oil over medium heat.
5. Add ½ of the tomato mixture and tilt the pan to spread it.
6. Cook for about 5–7 minutes.
7. Place the remaining oil over the "omelet" and carefully flip it over.
8. Cook for about 4–5 minutes or until golden-brown.
9. Repeat with the remaining mixture.

Nutrition: Calories 214 Fats 1.4 g Cholesterol 0 mg Carbohydrates 37.7 g Fiber 4.4 g Protein 6.4 g

204. **Veggie Omelet**

Preparation Time: 15 minutes
Cooking Time: 5 minutes
Servings: 2
Ingredients:
- ¼ cup chickpeas flour
- 1/3 cup spring water
- ¼ teaspoon fresh basil
- ¼ teaspoon dried oregano
- ¼ teaspoon onion powder
- ¼ teaspoon cayenne powder
- ¼ teaspoon sea salt

- ¼ cup plum tomato, chopped
- ¼ cup fresh button mushrooms, chopped
- ¼ cup green bell pepper, seeded and chopped
- ¼ cup onion, chopped
- 1 teaspoon grapeseed oil

Directions:
1. In a bowl, add the flour, water, herbs, spices, and salt and mix well.
2. In another bowl, mix together the tomato, mushrooms, bell pepper, and onion.
3. In a skillet, heat the oil over medium heat.
4. Place the veggie mixture in the skillet and spread in an even layer.
5. Top with chickpea flour mixture evenly and cook for about 3–4 minutes.
6. Carefully flip the omelet and fold it over.
7. Cook for about 1 minute.
8. Remove from the heat and serve hot.

Nutrition: Calories 83 Fats 0.3 g Cholesterol 0 mg Carbohydrates 10.8 g Fiber 2.3 g Protein 3.4 g

205. **Spelt Waffles**

Preparation Time: 10 minutes
Cooking Time: 15 minutes
Servings: 3
Ingredients:
- 1½ cups whole spelt flour
- 2 tablespoons date
- 1½ tablespoons baking powder
- 1/8 teaspoon salt
- 1½ cups unsweetened hemp milk
- 1/3 cup grapeseed oil
- 1 teaspoon vanilla extract

Directions:
1. In a bowl, add the flour, date
2. , baking powder, and salt and mix well.
3. Add the hemp milk, oil, and vanilla extract, and mix until well combined.
4. Set aside for about 3–5 minutes.
5. Preheat the waffle iron.
6. Generously grease the waffle iron.
7. Place 1/3 of the mixture into preheated waffle iron and cook for about 4–5 minutes or until golden-brown.
8. Repeat with the remaining mixture.
9. Serve warm.

Nutrition: Calories 547 Fats 2.6 g Cholesterol 0 mg Carbohydrates 60 g Fiber 8.2 g Protein 9 g

206. Coconut Waffles

Preparation Time: 10 minutes
Cooking Time: 10 minutes
Servings: 2
Ingredients:

- ¾ cup chickpea flour
- ¼ cup unsweetened coconut flakes
- 6–8 walnuts, chopped
- 1–2 tablespoon date syrup
- 1 tablespoon bromide mix
- Pinch of sea salt
- ½ cup unsweetened hemp milk
- ½ cup spring water
- ½ teaspoon vanilla extract

Directions:

1. In a high-powered blender, put in all the Ingredients: and pulse until well combined.
2. Set aside for about 3–5 minutes.
3. Preheat the waffle iron.
4. Generously grease the waffle iron.
5. Place half of the mixture into preheated waffle iron and cook for about 4–5 minutes or until golden-brown.
6. Repeat with the remaining mixture.
7. Serve warm.

Nutrition: Calories 459 Fats 7.9 g Cholesterol 0 mg Carbohydrates 56.5 g Fiber 15.6 g Protein 18.9 g

207. Vegetable Soup

Preparation Time: 5 minutes
Cooking Time: 12 minutes
Serving: 2
Ingredients

- ½ of onion, peeled, cubed
- ½ of green bell pepper, chopped
- ½ of zucchini, grated
- 4 ounces sliced mushrooms, chopped
- ½ cup cherry tomatoes
- Extra:
- ¼ cup basil leaves
- 1 pack of spelt noodles, cooked
- ¼ teaspoon salt
- 1/8 teaspoon cayenne pepper
- ½ of key lime, juiced
- 1 tablespoon grapeseed oil
- 2 cups spring water

Directions

1. Take a medium saucepan, place it over medium heat, add oil and when hot, add onion and then cook for 3 minutes or more until tender.
2. Add cherry tomatoes, bell pepper, and mushrooms, stir until mixed, and then continue cooking for 3 minutes until soft.
3. Add grated zucchini, season with salt, cayenne pepper, pour in the water, and then bring the mixture to a boil.
4. Then switch heat to the low level, add cooked noodles and then simmer the soup for 5 minutes.
5. When done, ladle soup into two bowls, top with basil leaves, drizzle with lime juice and then serve.
6. Storage instructions:
7. Cool the soup, divide evenly between two meal prep containers, cover with a lid, and then store the containers in the refrigerator for up to 7 days.
8. Reheating instructions:
9. When ready to eat, reheat in the oven for 1 to 2 minutes until hot and then serve.

Nutrition: 265 Calories; 2 g Fats; 4 g Protein; 57 g Carbohydrates; 13.6 g Fiber;

208. Cucumber Gazpacho

Preparation Time: 5 minutes
Cooking Time: 0 minutes
Serving: 2
Ingredients

- 1 avocado, peeled, pitted, cold
- 1 cucumber, deseeded, unpeeled, cold
- ½ cup basil leaves, cold
- ½ of key lime, juiced
- 2 cups spring water, chilled
- Extra:
- 1 ½ teaspoon sea salt

Directions

1. Place all the ingredients into the jar of a high-speed food processor or blender and then pulse until smooth.
2. Tip the soup into a medium bowl and then chill for a minimum of 1 hour.
3. Divide the soup evenly between two bowls, top with some more basil and then serve.
4. Storage instructions:
5. Divide the gazpacho evenly between two meal prep containers, cover with a lid, and then store the containers in the refrigerator for up to 7 days.

Nutrition: 190 Calories; 15 g Fats; 4 g Protein; 15 g Carbohydrates; 6 g Fiber;

209. Raw Green Veggie Soup

Preparation Time: 5 minutes
Cooking Time: 5 minutes
Servings: 1
Ingredients:

- 1 avocado
- 1 zucchini, chopped
- 2 celery stalks, chopped
- 2 cups spinach
- 1/4 cup parsley, fresh
- 2 sliced green peppers
- 1/8 onion, chopped
- 1 garlic clove
- 1/4 cup almonds, soak overnight, and rinse
- Salt to taste
- 1-1/2 cup water
- 1 lemon juice
- Diced watermelon radish for garnish

Directions:

1. Add all the ingredients in a food processor except salt.
2. Pulse until smooth or until the desired consistency is desired.
3. Pour the soup in a saucepan to warm a little bit before seasoning with salt and squeezed lemon.
4. Garnish with watermelon radish and enjoy.

Nutrition: Calories: 48.9, Fat: 0.4g, Carbohydrates: 10.6g, Protein: 3.1g, Fiber: 3.9g

210. Butternut Pumpkin Soup

Preparation Time: 5 minutes
Cooking Time: 15 minutes
Serving: 2
Ingredients:

- 2 medium butternut squash, peeled, deseeded, chopped
- 1 medium white onion, peeled, chopped
- 2 cups soft-jelly coconut milk
- Extra:
- 2/3 teaspoon sea salt
- 1 cup spring water

Directions:

1. Take a large saucepan, place it over medium-high heat, pour in water, and then bring it to a boil.
2. Stir in salt, and add vegetables and then cook for 5 to 10 minutes until vegetables turn tender.

3. Remove pan from heat, add milk and then puree by using an immersion blender until smooth.

Nutrition: 133.3 Calories; 4.8 g Fats; 2.1 g Protein; 23.6 g Carbohydrates; 1.3 g Fiber;

211. Sea Moss Gel

Preparation Time: 10 minutes
Cooking Time: 10 minutes
Servings: 16
Ingredients:

- 1 cup dried raw Irish sea moss
- 1–2 cups spring water

Directions:

1. In a large bowl of water, place sea moss, and with your hands, massage it to remove any visible dirt and debris.
2. Drain the sea moss and repeat this process once more.
3. In a large bowl, place the sea moss and cover with spring water.
4. Set aside at room temperature to soak for about 12–24 hours.
5. In a high-powered blender, add the sea moss along with the water and pulse until smooth.
6. Transfer the sea moss gel into an airtight container and refrigerate for at least 2 hours before serving.

Nutrition: Calories 2 Fats 0 g Cholesterol 0 mg Carbohydrates 0.6 g Fiber 0.1 g Protein 0.1 g

212. Elderberry-Infused Sea Moss Gel

Preparation Time: 15 minutes
Cooking Time: 30 minutes
Servings: 16
Ingredients:

- 1 cup sea moss
- 2½ cups spring water
- 2–3 tablespoons dried elderberries
- 1 (2–3-inch) piece fresh ginger

Directions:

1. In a large bowl of water, place sea moss, and with your hands, massage it to remove any visible dirt and debris.
2. Drain the sea moss and repeat this process once more.
3. In a large bowl, place the sea moss and add enough water to cover.

4. Set aside at room temperature to soak for about 12–24 hours.
5. Drain the sea moss and transfer onto a clean plate.
6. Discard the soaking water.
7. In a small saucepan, add spring water, elderberries, and ginger and bring to a boil.
8. Now, adjust the heat to low and simmer for about 25 minutes.
9. Remove the saucepan from heat and set aside to cool completely.
10. Strain the water.
11. In a high-powered blender, add the sea moss with about 1 cup of infused water and pulse until smooth.
12. Transfer the sea moss gel into an airtight container and refrigerate for at least 2 hours before serving.

Nutrition: Calories 4 Fats 0 g Cholesterol 0 mg Carbohydrates 1.1 g Fiber 0.2 g Protein 0.1 g

213. Sea Moss & Pineapple Smoothie

Preparation Time: 10 minutes
Cooking Time: 10 minutes
Servings: 2
Ingredients:
- 2 frozen bananas
- 1 cup fresh pineapple
- 2 teaspoons sea moss gel
- 1 cup unsweetened coconut milk
- ½ cup ice cubes

Directions:
1. In a high-powered blender, put all Ingredients: and pulse until creamy.
2. Place the smoothie into two serving glasses and serve.

Nutrition: Calories 327 Fats 15.1 g Cholesterol 0 mg Carbohydrates 41 g Fiber 4.2 g Protein 3.3 g

214. Green Sea Moss Smoothie

Preparation Time: 10 minutes
Cooking Time: 10 minutes
Servings: 2
Ingredients:
- 1½ cups fresh kale
- 1 green apple; peeled, cored, and chopped
- 1 burro banana, peeled
- 2 teaspoons sea moss gel
- 1 teaspoon chia seeds

- 1¼ cups spring water
- 1 cup ice cubes

Directions:
1. In a high-powered blender, put all Ingredients: and pulse until creamy.
2. Place the smoothie into two serving glasses and serve.

Nutrition: Calories 141 Fats 0.1 g Cholesterol 0 mg Carbohydrates 34.8 g Fiber 5.4 g Protein 2.7 g

215. Sea Moss Tea

Preparation Time: 5 minutes
Cooking Time: 5 minutes
Servings: 1
Ingredients:
- 1 cup boiling spring water
- 1 tablespoon sea moss gel
- 1 burdock tea bag
- 1 teaspoon agave nectar

Directions:
1. In a teapot, add boiling water and sea moss gel and stir to dissolve.
2. In the teapot, add the tea bag and steep, covered for 5 minutes.
3. Serve immediately.

Nutrition: Calories 22 Fats 0 g Cholesterol 0 mg Carbohydrates 5.9 g Fiber 0.4 g Protein 0.1 g

216. Spiced Sea Moss Tea

Preparation Time: 10 minutes
Cooking Time: 35 minutes
Servings: 4
Ingredients:
- 5–6 cups spring water
- 1 cup coconut cream
- 1 teaspoon fresh ginger root
- 1 cinnamon stick
- 3–5 whole cloves
- ½ teaspoon nutmeg
- ¼ cup sea moss gel
- 4 teaspoons agave nectar

Directions:
1. In a saucepan, add water, coconut cream, ginger, and spices over medium heat and bring to a boil.
2. Now, adjust the heat to low and simmer for about 20–25 minutes.
3. Remove from the heat and strain the spiced tea into a teapot.

4. Add the sea moss gel and agave nectar and stir to dissolve completely.
5. Transfer into serving cups and serve immediately.

Nutrition: Calories 83 Fats 4.4 g Cholesterol 0 mg Carbohydrates 8.5 g Fiber 0.5 g Protein 0.7 g

217. Avocado Vegan Caprese Salad

Preparation Time: 5 minutes
Cooking Time: 5 minutes
Servings: 1
Ingredients:
- 1 1/2 teaspoons balsamic vinegar
- Generous pinch of sugar
- 3 slices fresh vegan cheese
- Fresh basil leaves
- 2 cups fresh arugula
- 2-3 campari or cocktail style tomatoes sliced
- 1/2 avocado pitted and sliced
- 1 tablespoon extra-virgin olive oil
- Kosher salt and freshly ground black pepper

Directions:
1. In a serving bowl, add the arugula, onion, avocado slices, and vegan cheese.
2. Fill with leaves of broken or slivered basil.
3. With the balsamic vinegar, sugar, whisk the extra virgin olive oil in a small bowl and season with kosher salt and freshly ground black pepper to taste and pour over the salad.
4. Throw coat and serve.

Nutrition: Calories 214 Fats 1.4 g Cholesterol 0 mg Carbohydrates 37.7 g Fiber 4.4 g Protein 6.4 g

218. Spelt Bread with Avocado Oil

Preparation Time: 15 minutes
Cooking Time: 50 minutes
Servings: 8
Ingredients:
- 3 cups spelt flour
- 1 teaspoon baking soda
- 1 teaspoon sea salt
- 2 tablespoons date syrup
- 2½ tablespoons avocado oil
- 1 cup plus 1 tablespoon spring water

Directions:
1. Preheat your oven to 375°F.
2. Lightly flour a baking sheet.
3. In a bowl, put flour, baking soda, and salt and mix well.
4. In another small bowl, add the date syrup, oil, and water and mix well.
5. Add the oil mixture into the bowl of flour mixture and mix until a smooth dough forms.
6. Place the dough onto a lightly floured surface and with your hands, gently knead the dough for about 2–3 minutes.
7. With your hands, make a 6-inch-round loaf from dough.
8. Arrange the loaf onto the prepared baking sheet and with a sharp knife, score the top in a semicircle.
9. Bake for approximately 50 minutes or until a wooden skewer inserted in the center of loaf comes out clean.
10. Remove from oven and place the baking sheet onto a wire rack to cool for at least 10 minutes.
11. Carefully invert the bread onto the rack to cool completely before serving.
12. With a knife, cut the bread loaf into desired-sized slices and serve.

Nutrition: Calories 172 Fats 0.3 g Cholesterol 0 mg Carbohydrates 36.5 g Fiber 9.7 g Protein 6.7 g

219. Fruit Punch Alkaline

Preparation Time: 10 minutes
Cooking Time: 10 minutes
Servings: 2
Ingredients:

- 1 cup frozen Peaches,
- 1 cup frozen Blueberries,
- 1/2 to 1 cup Agave*
- 1 cup frozen Cherries,
- 1 cup frozen Strawberries,
- 6 cups of Spring Water
- Ice
- Equipment
- Fine Strainer
- Blender

Directions:

1. In a blender, incorporate fruit, 1/2 cup of agave & 2 cups of spring water & combine for around thirty seconds.
2. To extract unwanted seeds, pour the mixture through the strainer. (Optional step)
3. To a wide pitcher, put the combination, ice, and the remaining four cups of water & combine.
4. Cherish your Fruit Punch.

Nutrition: Calories 344, Fat 12, Fiber 5, Carbohydrates 35, Protein 56

LUNCH

220. Zucchini Cauliflower Fritters

Preparation Time: 5 Minutes
Cooking Time: 15 Minutes
Servings: 2
Ingredients:
- ¼ Head of cauliflower, chopped (roughly 1 ½ cups)
- 1 Tablespoon coconut oil
- 1/8 cup coconut flour
- 1 Medium zucchini; grated
- Black pepper and sea salt to taste

Directions:
1. Steam the cauliflower until just for tender, for 3 to 5 minutes.
2. Add cauliflower to your food processor and process on high power until broken down into very small chunks (ensure it's not mashed).
3. Squeeze the moisture as much as possible from the grated veggies using a nut milk bag or dishtowel.
4. Transfer to a large bowl along with the grated zucchini and add flour coconut flour followed by pepper, salt, and any seasonings you desire; combine well.
5. Make four small-sized patties from the mixture.
6. Now, over moderate heat in a large pan; heat one Tablespoon of coconut oil.
7. Work in batches and cook the fritters for 2 to 3 minutes per side.
8. The cooked fritters can be served with some dipping sauce of your choice on the side.

Nutrition:
- Calories: 112
- Fats: 8g
- Carbs: 5.6g
- Proteins: 2.1g

221. Eggless Salad

Preparation Time: 5 Minutes
Cooking Time: 5 Minutes
Servings: 4
Ingredients:
- 1 Stalk celery, chopped
- Vegan mayonnaise, as required
- 1-pound extra-firm tofu
- 2 Tablespoons onions, minced
- Pepper and salt to taste

Directions:

1. Mash the tofu into a chunky texture, just like an egg salad.
2. Add mayonnaise until you get your desired consistency.
3. Add in the leftover ingredients; stir well.
4. Serve on keto pitas or keto bread with vegetables, and enjoy.

Nutrition:
- Calories: 117
- Fats: 7.8
- Carbs: 2.8g
- Proteins: 16g

222. Mouth-Watering Guacamole

Preparation Time: 5 Minutes
Cooking Time: 0 Minutes
Servings: 6
Ingredients:
- 3 Avocados, pitted
- ¼ Cup cilantro, freshly chopped, plus more for garnish
- Juice of 2 limes
- ½ Teaspoon kosher salt
- 1 small jalapeño, minced
- ½ Small white onion, finely chopped

Directions:
1. Combine avocados with cilantro, lime juice, jalapeño, onion, and salt in a large-sized mixing bowl; mix well.
2. Give the ingredients a good stir and then slowly turn the bowl, running a fork through the avocados.
3. Once you get your desired level of consistency, immediately season it with more salt, if required.
4. Just before serving, feel free to garnish your recipe with fresher cilantro.

Nutrition:
- Calories: 165
- Fat: 15g
- Carbs: 9.5g
- Proteins: 2.1g

223. Roasted Green Beans

Preparation Time: 5 Minutes
Cooking Time: 30 Minutes
Servings: 4
Ingredients:
- 3 cups green beans, raw, trimmed
- 1 Tablespoon Italian seasoning

- 2 Tablespoons olive oil
- Ground black pepper and kosher salt to taste
- 4 Tablespoons pumpkin seeds

Directions:
1. Combine green beans with olive oil and seasonings in a large bowl; toss to coat.
2. Spread them out on a roasting pan or cookie sheet, preferably large-sized.
3. Roast in the oven for 20 minutes at 400°F.
4. Remove; give everything a good stir.
5. Place the cookie sheet again into the oven and roast for ten more minutes.
6. Remove.
7. Sprinkle pumpkin seeds, serve warm and enjoy.

Nutrition:
- Calories: 155
- Fats: 12g
- Carbs: 8.7g
- Proteins: 6.4g

224. Fried Tofu

Preparation Time: 10 Minutes
Cooking Time: 6 Minutes
Servings: 4

Ingredients:
- 1 Teaspoon seasoning
- 3 Tablespoons tamari or soya sauce
- 1 Package extra-firm tofu (350g)
- ¼ Cup Nutritional yeast
- 1 Tablespoon olive oil

Directions:
1. Lightly coat a large, non-stick pan with some oil.
2. Put soy sauce (tamari) in a medium-sized mixing bowl.
3. Mix the spices with the yeast in a separate bowl.
4. Slice the tofu into slices, approximately ¼.
5. Dip the tofu pieces in the tamari and then into the yeast mixture.
6. Fry until golden, for 2 to 3 minutes; flip and let the other side become brown for 2 to 3 more minutes.
7. If required, add a bit of oil.

Nutrition:
- Calories: 139
- Fats: 8.6
- Carbs: 5.1g

- Proteins: 12.1g

225. Curry Roasted Cauliflower

Preparation Time: 5 Minutes
Cooking Time: 15 Minutes
Servings: 2

Ingredients:
- 1/2-pound Cauliflower, approximately a large head; remove the outer leaves, cut into half and then cut out and discard the core; cutting it further into bite-sized pieces
- 2 Tablespoons nuts; any of your favorites
- 1 ½ Teaspoon curry powder
- 1 Tablespoon plus 1 teaspoon extra-virgin olive oil
- 2 teaspoons lemon juice, fresh
- 1 teaspoon kosher salt

Directions:
1. Preheat your oven to 425°F.
2. Toss the cauliflower pieces with olive oil in a large bowl until evenly coated. Sprinkle with curry powder and salt.
3. Give everything a good toss until nicely coated.
4. Spread them out on a large-sized rimmed baking sheet, preferably in an even layer, and transfer them to the preheated oven.
5. Roast for 8 to 10 minutes until the bottom is starting to turn brown.
6. Turn them over and continue to roast for 5 to 7 more minutes until fork-tender.
7. Place them in the bowl again
8. Toss with freshly squeezed lemon juice and your favorite nuts.
9. Serve immediately and enjoy.

Nutrition:
- Calories: 188
- Fats: 16.7g
- Carbs: 8.1g
- Proteins: 6.3g

226. Roasted Brussels Sprouts with Pecans and Almond Butter

Preparation Time: 5 Minutes
Cooking Time: 35 Minutes
Servings: 4

Ingredients:
- 1 Pound Brussels sprouts, fresh; ends trimmed
- ¼ cup almond butter
- 2 Tablespoons olive oil
- ½ cup pecans, chopped or to taste
- Fresh ground black pepper and salt to taste

Directions:
1. Using a pastry brush, lightly coat a large-sized roasting pan with one tablespoon of olive oil and preheat your oven to 350°F in advance.
2. Cut each Brussels sprout lengthwise into halves or fourths.
3. Chop the pecans using a sharp knife and measure the desired amount out.
4. Put the chopped pecans and Brussels sprouts into a large-sized plastic bowl and toss with one tablespoon olive oil.
5. Generously season with fresh ground black pepper and salt to taste.
6. Arrange the pecans and brussels sprouts in a single layer on a roasting pan.
7. Roast in the preheated oven until the sprouts begin to brown on the edges and are fork-tender for 30 to 35 minutes, stirring several times during the cooking process.
8. Just before serving, toss the cooked pecans and brussels sprouts with almond butter.
9. Serve hot and enjoy.

Nutrition:
- Calories: 175
- Fats: 23.5g
- Carbs: 11g
- Proteins: 7.6g

227. Asparagus Frittata

Preparation Time: 10 Minutes
Cooking Time: 15 Minutes
Servings: 4

Ingredients:
- ¼ Cup onion chopped
- A drizzle of olive oil
- 1-pound asparagus spears cut into 1-inch pieces
- Salt and ground black pepper to taste
- 4 Eggs, whisked
- 1 Cup cheddar cheese, grated

Directions:
1. Heat a pan with oil over medium heat.
2. Add onions, and stir-fry for 3 minutes.
3. Add asparagus and stir-fry for 6 minutes.
4. Add eggs and stir-fry for 3 minutes.
5. Add salt, pepper, and sprinkle with cheese.
6. Place in the oven and broil for 3 minutes.
7. Divide frittata between plates and serve.

Nutrition:
- Calories: 202
- Fats: 13.3g
- Carbs: 5.8g
- Proteins: 15.1g

228. Bell Peppers Soup

Preparation Time: 10 Minutes
Cooking Time: 15 Minutes
Servings: 6

Ingredients:
- 12 Roasted bell peppers, seeded and chopped
- 2 Tablespoons olive oil
- 2 Garlic cloves minced
- 30 Ounces vegetable stock
- Salt and black pepper to taste
- 6 Ounces water
- 2/3 cup Heavy cream
- 1 Onion chopped
- ¼ cup parmesan cheese grated
- 2 Celery stalks chopped

Directions:
1. Heat a saucepan with oil over medium heat.
2. Add onion, garlic, celery, salt, and pepper.
3. Stir-fry for 8 minutes.
4. Add water, bell peppers, stock, stir, and bring to a boil.
5. Cover on lower heat, and simmer for 5 minutes.
6. Remove from heat and blend with a hand mixer.
7. Then adjust seasoning, and add cream.
8. Stir and bring to a boil.
9. Remove from the heat and serve on bowls.
10. Sprinkle with Parmesan and serve.

Nutrition:
- Calories: 155
- Fats: 12g
- Carbs: 8.6g
- Proteins: 4.7g

229. Radish Hash Browns

Preparation Time: 10 Minutes
Cooking Time: 10 Minutes
Servings: 4

Ingredients:

- ½ Teaspoon onion powder
- 1 Pound, radishes shredded
- ½ Teaspoon garlic powder
- Salt and ground black pepper to taste
- 4 Eggs
- 1/3 Cup parmesan cheese grated

Directions:

1. In a bowl, mix radishes with salt, pepper, onion, garlic powder, eggs, Parmesan cheese, and mix well.
2. Spread on a lined baking sheet.
3. Place in an oven at 375°F and bake for 10 minutes.
4. Serve.

Nutrition:

- Calories: 104
- Fats: 6g
- Carbs: 4.5g
- Proteins: 8.6g

230. Celery Soup

Preparation Time: 10 Minutes
Cooking Time: 30 Minutes
Servings: 6

Ingredients:

- 1 Bunch celery chopped
- 1 Fresh bunch parsley chopped
- 2 Fresh mint bunches chopped
- 1 Onion chopped
- 4 Garlic cloves minced
- Salt and ground black pepper to taste
- 3 Dried Persian lemons pricked with a fork
- 2 cups water
- 4 Tablespoons olive oil

Directions:

1. Heat a saucepan with oil over medium heat.
2. Add onion, garlic, and green onions.
3. Stir and cook for 6 minutes.

4. Add Persian lemons, celery, salt, pepper, water, stir, cover the pan, and simmer on medium heat for 20 minutes.
5. Add parsley and mint, stir, and cook for 10 minutes.
6. Blend with a hand mixer and serve.

Nutrition:

- Calories: 100
- Fats: 9.5g
- Carbs: 4.4g
- Proteins: 1g

231. Spring Greens Soup

Preparation Time: 10 Minutes
Cooking Time: 30 Minutes
Servings: 4

Ingredients:

- 2 Cups mustard greens chopped
- 2 Cups collard greens chopped
- 4 cups vegetable stock
- 1 Onion chopped
- Salt and ground black pepper to taste
- 2 Tablespoons coconut aminos
- 2 teaspoons grated fresh ginger

Directions:

5. Put the stock into a saucepan and bring to a simmer over medium heat.
6. Add ginger, coconut aminos, salt, pepper, onion, mustard, and collard greens. Stir, cover, and cook for 30 minutes.
7. Remove from the heat.
8. Blend the soup with a hand mixer.
9. Serve.

Nutrition:

- Calories: 35
- Fats: 1g
- Carbs: 7g
- Proteins: 2g

232. Alfalfa Sprouts Salad

Preparation Time: 10 Minutes
Cooking Time: 10 Minutes
Servings: 4

Ingredients:

- 1 ½ Teaspoon dark sesame oil
- 4 Cups of alfalfa sprouts
- Salt and ground black pepper to taste
- 1 ½ Teaspoon grapeseed oil
- ¼ Cup coconut yogurt

Directions:
1. In a bowl, mix sprouts with yogurt, grape seed oil, sesame oil, salt, and pepper. Toss to coat and serve.

Nutrition:
- Calories: 83
- Fats: 7.6g
- Carbs: 3.4g
- Proteins: 1.6g

233. Eggplant Stew

Preparation Time: 10 Minutes
Cooking Time: 30 Minutes
Servings: 4

Ingredients:
- 1 Onion, chopped
- 2 Garlic cloves, chopped
- 1 Fresh parsley bunch, chopped
- Salt and black pepper to taste
- 1 teaspoon dried oregano
- 2 Eggplants cut into chunks
- 2 Tablespoons olive oil
- 2 Tablespoons capers chopped
- 12 Green olives, pitted and sliced
- 5 Tomatoes chopped
- 3 Tablespoons herb vinegar

Directions:
- In a saucepan, heat oil over medium heat.
- Add oregano, eggplant, salt, pepper, and stir-fry for 5 minutes.
- Add parsley, onion, garlic, and stir-fry for 4 minutes.
- Add tomatoes, vinegar, olives, capers, and stir-fry for 15 minutes.
- Adjust seasoning and stir.
- Serve.

Nutrition:
- Calories: 280
- Fats: 17.9g

- Carbs: 8.4g
- Proteins: 5.4g

234. Zucchini Salad

Preparation Time: 10 Minutes
Cooking Time: 10 Minutes
Servings: 6

Ingredients:
- 2 Tablespoons butter or olive oil
- 3 oz. Celery stalks, finely sliced
- 2 oz. Chopped scallions
- 1 cup mayonnaise
- 2 Pounds zucchini
- 3 oz. Celery stalks, finely sliced
- 2 oz. Chopped scallions
- 1 cup mayonnaise
- 2 Tablespoons. fresh chives, finely chopped
- ½ Tablespoons Dijon Mustard
- Sea Salt
- Pepper

Directions:
- Peel and cut the zucchini into pieces that are about half an inch thick. Use a spoon to remove the seeds.
- Place in a colander and add salt. Leave for 5 – 10 minutes, and then cautiously press out the water.
- Fry the cubes in butter for a couple of minutes over medium heat. They should not brown, just slightly soften.
- Set aside to cool.
- Mix the other ingredients in a large bowl and add the zucchini once it's cool.
- Tip: You can prepare the salad 1-2 days ahead of time; the flavors only enhance with time. You can also add a chopped hard-boiled egg.

Nutrition:
- Calories: 312
- Fats: 32g
- Carbs: 4g
- Proteins: 3g

235. Loaded Baked Cauliflower

Preparation Time: 10 Minutes
Cooking Time: 30 Minutes
Servings: 2

Ingredients:
- 4 Ounces bacon
- 1-pound cauliflower
- 2/3 cup sour cream
- ½ Pound cheddar cheese, shredded
- 2 Tablespoons chives, finely chopped
- 1Teaspoon garlic powder
- Sea salt
- Freshly ground pepper

Directions:
- Preheat oven to 350°F.
- Chop the bacon into small pieces.
- Fry until crispy in a hot frying pan.
- Reserve the fat for serving.
- Break the cauliflower into florets.
- Boil until soft in lightly salted water. Drain completely.
- Chop the cauliflower roughly. Add sour cream and garlic powder.
- Combine well with ¾ of the cheese and most of the finely chopped chives.
- Salt and pepper
- Place in a baking dish and top with the rest of the cheese.
- Bake in the oven for 10 – 15 minutes or until the cheese has melted.
- Top with the bacon, the rest of the chives, and the bacon fat. Enjoy.

Nutrition:
- Calories: 614
- Fats: 49g
- Carbs: 10g
- Proteins: 30g

236. Cabbage Hash Browns

Preparation Time: 10 Minutes
Cooking Time: 12 Minutes
Servings: 2

Ingredients:
- 1 ½ Cup shredded cabbage
- 2 slices of bacon
- ½ Teaspoon garlic powder
- 1 Egg
- 1 Tablespoon coconut oil
- ½ Teaspoon salt
- 1/8 teaspoon ground black pepper

Directions:
- Crack the egg in a bowl, add garlic powder, black pepper, and salt, whisk well, add cabbage, and toss until well mixed and shape the mixture into four patties.
- Take a large skillet pan, place it over medium heat, add oil, and when hot, add patties in it and cook for 3 minutes per side until golden brown.
- Transfer hash browns to a plate, then add bacon into the pan and cook for 5 minutes until crispy.
- Serve hash browns with bacon.

Nutrition:
- Calories: 336
- Fats: 29.5g
- Carbs: 1g
- Fiber: 0.8g
- Proteins: 16g

237. Cauliflower Hash Brown

Preparation Time: 10 Minutes
Cooking Time: 18 Minutes
Servings: 2

Ingredients:
- ¾ Cup grated cauliflower
- 2 slices of bacon
- ½ Teaspoon garlic powder
- 1 large egg white

Seasoning:
- 1 Tablespoon coconut oil
- ½ Teaspoon salt

- 1/8 teaspoon ground black pepper

Directions:

1. Place grated cauliflower in a heatproof bowl, cover with plastic wrap, poke some holes in it with a fork and then microwave for 3 minutes until tender.

2. Let steamed cauliflower cool for 10 minutes, then wrap in a cheesecloth and squeeze well to drain moisture as much as possible.
3. Crack the egg in a bowl, add garlic powder, black pepper, and salt, whisk well, then add cauliflower and toss until well mixed and a sticky mixture forms.
4. Take a large skillet pan, place it over medium heat, add oil, and when hot, drop cauliflower mixture on it, press lightly to form hash brown patties, and cook for 3 to 4 minutes per side until browned.
5. Transfer hash browns to a plate, then add bacon into the pan and cook for 5 minutes until crispy.
6. Serve hash browns with bacon.

Nutrition:
- Calories: 347
- Fats: 31g
- Carbs: 1.2g
- Fiber 0.5g
- Proteins: 15.6g

28-Day Meal Plan

Week 1

	Monday	Tuesday	Wednesday	Thursday	Friday	Saturday	Sunday
Breakfast	Moringa Leaves Mung Beans Soup	Healthy Oatmeal	Morning Ritual Smoothie	Smokey Sweet Beans & Tomatoes	Healthy Oatmeal Breakfast	Liver Detox Smoothie	High-Protein French Toast
Lunch	Lentil Kebab Bowl with Turmeric Tahini Sauce	Buffalo Blue Cheese Club	Pappardelle with Spiced Meat Sauce	Zucchini Lasagna with Cashew Cheese Pesto	Asian Beef & Mango Salad with Cashews	Garlic Herb Zucchini Noodles with Lobster	Turkey & Farro Zucchini Boats
Dinner	Chipotle Chicken Burgers along with Ginger Lime Aioli & Cucumber Salad	Coconut Chicken Corn Chowder	Kale Salad with Sweet Potato & Sausage	Herbed Skirt Steak Tacos with Beet & Fresno Chile Salsa	Coconut Shrimp Stir-Fry	Biryani-Style Chicken Kamut	Za'atar Roasted Salmon with Warm Quinoa Salad & Yogurt Sauce

Week 2

	Monday	Tuesday	Wednesday	Thursday	Friday	Saturday	Sunday
Breakfast	Broccoli Salad	Classic Eggs Benedict with Lemon Basil Hollandaise	Blueberry Smoothie	Fried Egg & Greens	Sweet Potato Pie Smoothie Bowl	Cornmeal Pancakes with Black Bean Salsa & Cilantro Yogurt	Southwestern-Style Black Bean Burritos
Lunch	Easiest, Quickest Sirloin Beef Wraps	Indian Red Lentils with Rice & Hard-Boiled Eggs	Lentil Kebab Bowl with Turmeric Tahini Sauce	Buffalo Blue Cheese Club	Pappardelle with Spiced Meat Sauce	Zucchini Lasagna with Cashew Cheese Pesto	Asian Beef & Mango Salad with Cashews
Dinner	Ginger Chicken Fajitas with Cashew Sour Cream	Mango Mint Green tea (Iced)	Persian-Style Spinach & Herb Sauté with Eggs	Chipotle Chicken Burgers along with Ginger Lime Aioli & Cucumber Salad	Coconut Chicken Corn Chowder	Kale Salad with Sweet Potato & Sausage	Herbed Skirt Steak Tacos with Beet & Fresno Chile Salsa

Week 3

¤	Monday ¤	Tuesday ¤	Wednesday ¤	Thursday ¤	Friday ¤	Saturday ¤	Sunday ¤
Breakfast ¤	Fruit Yogurt Parfait ¤	Peanut Butter Maple Banana Muffins¶ ¤	Moringa Leaves Mung Beans Soup ¤	Healthy Oatmeal ¤	Morning Ritual Smoothie¶ ¤	Smokey Sweet Beans & Tomatoes¶ ¤	Healthy Oatmeal Breakfast¶ ¤
Lunch ¤	Garlic Herb Zucchini Noodles with Lobster ¤	Turkey & Farro Zucchini Boats ¤	Indian Red Lentils with Rice & Hard-Boiled Eggs ¤	Easiest, Quickest Sirloin Beef Wraps ¤	Buffalo Blue Cheese Club ¤	Lentil Kebab Bowl with Turmeric Tahini Sauce ¤	Zucchini Lasagna with Cashew ¤
Dinner ¤	Biryani-Style Chicken Kamut ¤	Za'atar Roasted Salmon with Warm Quinoa Salad & Yogurt Sauce¶ ¤	Ginger Chicken Fajitas with Cashew Sour Cream¶ ¤	Chicken Paillards with Porcini, Red Wine & Butter Sauce¶ ¤	Mango Mint Green tea (Iced) ¤	Persian-Style Spinach & Herb Sauté with Eggs ¤	Chipotle Chicken Burgers along with Ginger Lime Aioli & Cucumber Salad ¤

Week 4

¤	Monday ¤	Tuesday ¤	Wednesday ¤	Thursday ¤	Friday ¤	Saturday ¤	Sunday ¤
Breakfast ¤	Blueberry Smoothie¶ ¤	Classic Eggs Benedict with Lemon Basil Hollandaise¶ ¤	Fried Egg & Greens ¤	Southwestern-Style Black Bean Burritos¶ ¤	Cornmeal Pancakes with Black Bean Salsa & Cilantro Yogurt¶ ¤	Sweet Potato Pie Smoothie Bowl¶ ¤	Broccoli Salad ¤
Lunch ¤	Pappardelle with Spiced Meat Sauce ¤	Asian Beef & Mango Salad with Cashews ¤	Garlic Herb Zucchini Noodles with Lobster ¤	Turkey & Farro Zucchini Boats ¤	Indian Red Lentils with Rice & Hard-Boiled Eggs ¤	Zucchini Lasagna with Cashew ¤	Buffalo Blue Cheese Club ¤
Dinner ¤	Kale Salad with Sweet Potato & Sausage¶ ¤	Herbed Skirt Steak Tacos with Beet & Fresno Chile Salsa¶ ¤	Coconut Shrimp Stir-Fry ¤	Biryani-Style Chicken Kamut¶ ¤	Za'atar Roasted Salmon with Warm Quinoa Salad & Yogurt Sauce¶	Chicken Paillards with Porcini, Red Wine & Butter Sauce ¤	Mango Mint Green tea (Iced) ¶ ¤

Conclusion

The liver is the body's biggest gland, and it stores nutrients and neutralizes toxic substances. The liver is known as the "central laboratory" of the body since it is involved in various metabolic activities, both catabolic and anabolic. If you have liver disease, it may impact all your organs, including your liver cells, bile ducts, blood vessels, blood vessels, and lymph vessels. Toxins, medications, infections, blood supply problems, and other illnesses may harm the liver. For a long time, diet therapy has been a component of treating liver disease.

Fatty liver disease causes a reduction in liver function. Obesity is a frequent contributor to the development of cirrhosis. Many persons with fatty liver disease discover that they can maintain a healthy weight while managing their symptoms.

Patients with chronic liver disease eat a typical diet with the addition of supplements as needed. Restrictions may be damaging; thus, they should be tailored to the person. The goal of treatment management should be to maintain a healthy protein and calorie intake while also correcting any nutritional deficits. This book covers all the diet recipes required for the liver's normal functioning.

56042801R00059